BUILD YOUR CASE

Developing Listening, Thinking,
and Speaking Skills in English

Rodney E. Kleber

 Addison-Wesley Publishing Company

Reading, Massachusetts
Menlo Park, California • New York
Don Mills, Ontario • Wokingham, England
Amsterdam • Bonn • Sydney • Singapore
Tokyo • Madrid • Bogota • Santiago
San Juan

A Publication of the World Language Division

Project Editor: Kathleen Sands-Boehmer
Manufacturing/Production: James W. Gibbons
Interior and Cover Design: Gary Fujiwara
Illustrations: Len Reno

ISBN 0-201-16527-9
    EFGHIJKLMN-AL-9987654321

Acknowledgments

"All Things Considered," National Public Radio. The radio reports in chapter 4 of this textbook were originally broadcast on January 22, 1985 on National Public Radio's daily news and information program "All Things Considered." Reproduced in print and on tape by permission of National Public Radio.

R. Leeper. Dual-perception illustration (younger woman/older woman) believed to be adapted from R. Leeper's "The Role of Motivation in Learning: A Study of the Phenomenon of Differential Motivation Control on the Utilization of Habits" in the *Journal of Genetic Psychology*, 1935, volume 46, pages 3–40.

Sylvia Plath. "Metaphors" from *The Collected Poems of Sylvia Plath*, edited by Ted Hughes. Copyright © by Ted Hughes. Reprinted by permission of Harper & Row, Publishers, Inc.

Paul Reps, editor. "A Parable," English version by Nyogen Senzaki and Paul Reps, from *Zen Flesh, Zen Bones*. Adaptation used by permission of Charles E. Tuttle Co., Inc., of Tokyo, Japan.

Shel Silverstein. "Boa Constrictor," words and music by Shel Silverstein. Copyright © 1962 by Hollis Music, Inc., New York, New York. Used by permission.

May Swenson. "Living Tenderly" from *To Mix with Time* by May Swenson. Copyright © 1963 by May Swenson. Reprinted by permission of the author.

To my wife,
DIANE LUCINSKI KLEBER
and my daughter,
ALLISON KLEBER

Contents

PREFACE

This book and its accompanying tape have developed from my belief that there should be both pleasure in learning and joy in language. The result, when those two things are combined, should be an even greater joy in language learning.

This material has also developed from my belief that English-as-a-second-language (ESL) students should be respected as whole people whose native intellectual abilities need to be addressed. This need is perhaps especially important for intermediate-to-advanced-level students, for whom the material is designed.

This material is furthermore a product of my respect for ESL teachers who do not want the humdrum and who seek the dynamic. Long may they thrive.

Most of all, this material is a product of opportunity, interest, response, and support provided by several special people. I wish to thank Bill Bliss, Father James S. Woods, Bill Biddle, and Karen L. Stiles for opportunities to begin and Anne L. Dow for repeated opportunities to experiment and develop.

I am grateful to Gunnar Gundersen for his interest in and use of the early, trial material. My gratitude also to Greg Kaminski for his continuing interest and friendship. My thanks to Karen Willeto for an important key and to Marci Matlock for her encouragement.

A hearty thanks to former students, TESOL conventioneers, and other colleagues who have tried out the working material and provided valuable feedback.

Special thanks to John and Mary Ann Boyd for their advice as textbook writers and publishers and to Ann Strunk and Kathleen Sands-Boehmer for their editorial guidance.

Enduring thanks to Steven J. Molinsky not just for his clear-sighted comments, but also for his personal and professional grace first, last, and always.

Greatest thanks of all to my wife, Diane, and daughter, Allison. They made and continue to make everything possible. Their patience, understanding, and love are the foundation of this work.

TO THE STUDENT

Build Your Case: Developing Listening, Thinking, and Speaking Skills in English is intended to be both fun and challenging for you. The main part of the title, *Build Your Case*, has three important meanings in the plan of this book. You will "build your case" (1) by developing solutions to mysteries, (2) by giving support for your ideas and opinions, and (3) by improving your overall English language ability. These three meanings are explained below.

1. Developing Solutions to Mysteries

First of all, the word "case" can refer to a story that has some question, problem, or mystery in it that you can have the pleasure of solving. When you "build your case," you are actually developing a solution to a problem—finding out *what* really happened, *who* was responsible, *why* someone did something, *how* something was done, *where* something is hidden, and so on. Sometimes there is only one question to answer, and sometimes there are several questions in a case. Answering these questions is an enjoyable process. You carefully consider all the background information, you pay particular attention to the really important pieces of information (called "clues") that lead to solutions, and you put the pieces together in order to understand the big picture—to find your solution!

The most famous solver of cases in world literature has been the detective Sherlock Holmes. This character and the friend who helped him, Dr. Watson, were created by the British author Sir Arthur Conan Doyle. Their first adventures appeared in print toward the end of the nineteenth century. However, because of the two characters' great popularity, movies, plays, and TV shows of their exploits and new stories by other authors have continued to appear right to the present. Their tradition is continued in this book.

There are some important differences in the stories you will encounter in these pages. For one thing, because Holmes and Watson are timeless, they are brought into stories of the present and even of the future. We need their help with our problems of today and beyond today! More important, the stories in this book are ones that you will *listen to* far more than read. In fact, beyond listening, the stories will require that you *interact* with them and *think* about them carefully in order to understand them and develop solutions to the problems in them.

2. Giving Support for Your Ideas and Opinions

The second important meaning of "build your case" is for you to give support for your ideas and opinions. Not only will you practice giving support (facts, details, and reasons) for your solutions to the mysteries, you will also practice giving similar support for what you say in *discussions* and *presentations.* As you proceed through this book, you will learn how to represent yourself and your ideas effectively in English.

3. Improving Your Overall English Language Ability

The last and most important meaning of "build your case" is for you to improve your individual ability with the English language in general. You will do this by *working on* listening, thinking, and speaking skills in English—in the process working on vocabulary development as an important part of all three skill areas. And you will also improve your ability by *playing with, manipulating, and enjoying* English as native speakers do. The idea of play is added to the idea of work in order to give balance to your learning—in order to appeal to both the affective (feeling) and cognitive (thinking) parts of your personality. The goal, quite simply, is to help you learn better by learning more enjoyably. As Sherlock Holmes might say, in a slight alteration of his usual statement, "It's elementary, my dear student!" Your own positive approach to the stories and exercises is, of course, essential; it will help you develop the strongest possible case for yourself in English.

TO THE TEACHER

Overview

Build Your Case: Developing Listening, Thinking, and Speaking Skills in English is intended for comprehensive or supplemental use in what we ESL teachers traditionally refer to as listening and speaking skills development. This book, however, seeks to take a fresh approach in several respects. First of all, pleasure listening is the starting point. Language professionals and nonprofessionals alike have long recognized the positive effects that pleasure reading has on language acquisition, so this book has adopted the idea of using engaging stories for listening purposes. The actual method of engagement is the presentation of a game, problem, or mystery for students to respond to or interact with. The follow-up exercises work in a similar way. James Moffett and Betty Jane Wagner provide a well stated rationale for this "game" procedure:

> A game context can permit focusing on substructures of the language . . . without violating communication integrity, because games frankly substitute rules for the sender-receiver-message relations as a basis for making decisions. Most games are social, of course, and require students to interact. The interaction entailed in playing such valuable games for their own sake also generates a lot of very good discussion along the way. (*Student-Centered Language Arts and Reading, K-13: A Handbook for Teachers*, 2d ed. Boston: Houghton Mifflin Company, 1976, 31)

A second aspect of this book's fresh approach, as the subtitle suggests, is its emphasis on thinking as an inseparable part of the listening and thinking process. Moreover, students will think at increasingly higher levels as they proceed through the material. The general concern for both the cognitive and the affective domains that is evident in the book is due, in good part, to the influence of *The Taxonomy of Educational Objectives*, edited by Benjamin S. Bloom. *Build Your Case* thus respects and values students' native intellectual abilities and seeks to address their cognitive and affective learning needs.

Third, this book presents specific points in listening and speaking for students to practice and develop both within the book and also outside it. By "outside it," I mean in their other studies and in their daily lives. In other words, students gain the specific means for improving their ability to operate in English both in class and on their own.

Fourth, this book functionally integrates other language and study skill areas such as reading, writing, note taking, and especially vocabulary development. The reading parts support the listening, thinking, and speaking activities. Similarly, the writing parts help crystallize students' thinking and aid their speaking. Note taking is an important skill in itself and helps ensure that dependency on full-scale reading and writing does not occur. Vocabulary development aids comprehension and language production generally.

The vocabulary component deserves additional comment as a special aspect of the book. The way the component works is *not* to have students memorize isolated words, but, instead, to provide them with the opportunity to play with, manipulate, and enjoy English in a way that will help them increase their appreciation and command of it. In other words, the object is for them to gain a feel for English similar to the feel they have for their first language. Thus, you will find such things as humor, word play, word games, euphemisms, general and specific language, denotations and connotations, idioms, two-word verbs, similes and metaphors, riddles, advertising language, and ethical teasers integrated in the cases and especially in the exercises.

Cases and Questions

The cases lead students to think more in English. At the same time, they are all readily solvable. The questions that immediately follow the cases help students to focus on the important details in the stories, to make sure of their basic understanding of the facts, and to think about the information and solve the cases.

You may have your students go to the questions before, during, or after the working out of a solution to a case. Reading the questions beforehand can help students focus their attention and thinking. Going through the questions while working on a case can aid the working process. Answering them afterwards is useful for summarizing a case and for gaining further discussion practice. How you use the questions will depend on the case, your students, and your purpose at a particular time.

The cases also deal with the listening skills that are the organizing principle for the work. Two chapters address each skill, with the exception of summarizing and inferring, which receive three chapters each because of their demanding nature (inferring even extends into a fourth chapter because of ties with anticipating as

a listening skill). At the same time, the skills that first appear in earlier parts of the book are also practiced in later parts. In general, the development of the listening skill material is not in strictly linear form or in isolated bits (that would be artificial, if at all possible). Instead, there is both a progression and a natural integration.

There is also a purposeful variety in the cases and in the way students are to interact with them. Two cases require that students actually take the roles of characters in the stories. For those two cases, you will assign numbers to your students so that they can learn their roles in the back of the book. You will also assign numbers so that students can locate additional clues to three other cases. The chapters, cases, and numbers are as follows.

* Chapter 2, *The Case of Hitting Rockbottom*: 6, 77, 58, 38, 91, 21, 12, 53, 30, 47, 65, 42, 86, 102, 33, 97, 24, 81, and 72. The first five roles are essential (and all that are really needed) for conducting the case. If you have more than nineteen students, assign number 72 to each of the students in excess of nineteen. You may also assign number 72 to several students, instead of assigning them the later numbers in the list above, if you wish to have more investigators, perhaps equaling the number of suspects to be questioned. In that way, you might provide even wider practice with the listening skill of repetition.

Note: Following the case, for exercise 3, you need to read the directions on page 180 for the students to draw the Rockbottom estate.

* Chapter 3, *The Case of the Missing Bracelet*: 99, 13, 35, 46, 74, 10, 50, 95, 89, 4, 61, 41, 22, 93, 27, 18, 69, 31, 85, 64, 105, and 56. If you have more than twenty-two students, assign some the same clue. If you have fewer than twenty-two students, you may assign some more than one clue.

* Chapter 7, *The Case of Marooned on the Moon*: 3, 26, 94, 57, 73, 88, 100, 68, 32, 54, 104, 15, 76, 37, 62, 8, 48, 82, 20, and 43. The first five roles are essential (and all that are really needed) for conducting the case. If you have more than twenty students, assign number 43 to each of the students in excess of twenty. After number 100 and through number 20 on the list, the total number of assignments must be odd, with a student or you yourself taking an extra role if necessary.

* Chapter 11, *The Case of the President's Hot Seat*: 16, 67, 29, 11, 45, 63, 39, 7, 92, 2, 103, 87, 19, 55, 36, 78, 59, 98, 70, 51, 83, and 25. If you have more than twenty-two students, assign some the same clue. If you have fewer than twenty-two students, you may assign some more than one clue.

* Chapter 12, *The Case of the Green Eyes, or "Isle Be Seeing You"*: 96, 40, 75, 34, 44, 52, 28, 49, 1, 17, 79, 23, 90, 66, 101, 9, 84, 5, 60, 106, 14, and 71. If you have more than twenty-two students, assign some the same clue. If you have fewer than twenty-two students, you may assign some more than one clue.

It is a good idea to have your students discuss how all of the clues fit the final solutions of the cases in chapters 3, 11, and 12. In that way, all of your students will have a chance to explain the cases, from the individual parts to the whole cases. It is also a good idea, for the same reason, to have your students discuss the important details and the behind-the-scenes actions of the other cases in the book. The questions that follow the cases can help guide your "wrapping-up" discussions.

The solutions to all of the cases are in the back of the book. Actually, three entire cases and part of a fourth one are open to interpretation and, what is really to the point, to discussion. Moreover, for all of the cases, getting the right solution is not what matters most. Instead, it is the process of listening, thinking, and speaking in English.

Exercises

Most of the exercises tie into the listening skills that, with the cases, head the chapters. Students gain practice with the skills by responding to material on tape or by interacting with other students. Many of the taped exercises are "conversational" in nature, involving authentic voices presenting authentic messages that your students will respond to.

Every chapter also includes a discussion exercise on subject matter from the chapter's introductory case or from elsewhere in the chapter. In addition, important information about participating in discussions appears in the odd-numbered chapters, and a "test your memory" review of the information follows in the even-numbered chapters.

Similarly, there is a content-related presentation exercise, with information about making presentations, in the even-numbered chapters. In chapter 7, the listening skill of summarizing and the work of presenting interconnect, and a note explains that you as the teacher may require spoken or written summaries of the presentations that students give in class thereafter. You may indeed wish to make summarizing or some other form of response (perhaps questions or comments) a part of the presentation activities in the book, beginning with this chapter, if not earlier.

A final word about the exercises: variety is a key element and not just for the sake of creating interest. Language enrichment and development, as well as practice with listening, thinking, and speaking skills, are a planned part of the exercises and of the material as a whole. More information about the language in the material appears in the Overview, above, and in the section immediately following.

Language

By design, this book uses language that is generally comprehensible for intermediate-to-advanced-level ESL students. As part of the design, students practice skills that help them deal with new language. Some problems in understanding may, quite naturally, still occur. You may wish to consider your own students' knowledge and abilities and determine if they would benefit from the preteaching of certain words in a case or in an exercise.

Teacher Preparation and Presentation

Your familiarity with the cases and exercises will enable you to guide your students' learning and to respond to any questions they might have as they interact with the material. The cases for chapters 2, 3, 7, 11, and 12 actually require that you follow the procedures described for them above.

With the tape that accompanies the book, you may wish to adjust pauses or replay material to set just the right pace for your students' learning. Generally speaking, sufficient pauses and replayings are in order because the object of the material is to help develop language ability, not to test it. At the same time, students should not become dependent on extended pauses or numerous replayings.

A good way to begin working and playing with *Build Your Case* is to have your students read "To the Student." That will orient them to the purposes of the book and to the Sherlock Holmes framework. After that, your readiness to enjoy the material with your students—to help them take pleasure in "cracking the code" of English—should lead to happy solutions over time. It's elementary, my dear colleague!

BUILD YOUR CASE

1 The Case of the Treasure Hunt, or "The Secret to Success"

Prelistening: The Situation

Sherlock Holmes became the most famous fictional detective in the world because he used his great analytical mind to solve the most difficult cases imaginable—although he himself usually referred to his solutions as being "elementary." The present case offers a unique twist since Holmes is not the solver, but actually the creator of the mystery. Here is the situation.

Multimillionaire Frederick J. Farnsworth has hired Holmes to create a special treasure hunt at Farnsworth University. The purpose of the treasure hunt is to help students prepare for the future. With that goal in mind, Holmes has named the treasure "The Secret to Success," and he has located it on the grounds of the university. What is the treasure? Nobody knows for sure, but everyone believes that it is something very valuable. Any student may look for the treasure by following the instructions below.

Instructions

1. Listen to Sherlock Holmes's directions on the tape.

2. Repeat each direction aloud after him while you look at the picture on the next page. Do not write or draw anything.

3. As you listen to the directions again, repeat them silently to yourself and draw the path that you follow in the picture.

According to Holmes, the solution to this case is quite elementary! And quite universal!

Questions

Answer these questions orally or in writing.

1. Look closely at the path that you drew in the picture. Does some part of your path look like an "X"? Explain.

2. Look at your path again. Does some part look like an "O"? Explain.

3. The speaker said that both an "X" and an "O" mark the spot of the treasure. What is the spot?

4. Do you think that there is any significance in the location of the treasure? Explain.

5. Do you think that there is any significance in the location of the treasure in relation to other things in the picture? Do these things suggest some important aspects of life? Explain.

6. Why do you think the directions took you to so many different places in the picture?

7. The treasure is hidden; that is, we cannot or do not see it. Which do you think is true: we cannot see it with our eyes, or we do not see it (think about it) in our minds?

8. The treasure is called "The Secret to Success." What do you think the treasure is?

9. How did repeating the directions help you locate the treasure?

Listening Skill: Repetition or Request for a Repetition

The information that you hear from another person may be something very important, like a name, a time, a price, a telephone number, an address, a direction, or something else. Repeating the information is often a good idea because you then make sure that you have heard it correctly. If you repeat it aloud incorrectly, your conversation partner will almost always give you the correct information again. If you did not hear the information well enough to understand it and repeat it, then requesting that the other person repeat it is a good listening practice.

If you use both repetition and request for a repetition, your conversation partner will know that you have been listening, and better communication will result.

Listen to the example on the tape.

Statement	Possible Responses
Hi, my name's Yoko.	1. Yoko. Pleased to meet you. I'm Ali.
	2. Your name's . . . Yoko. Nice meeting you. I'm Ali.
	3. Yoko?
	*4. Did you say your name's Yoko?
	5. Your name is . . . ?

6. I'm sorry, what's your name?

7. Your name is what? (informal, but said politely)

*8. Excuse me, what did you say your name is?

9. I'm sorry, I didn't catch your name.

10. I'm sorry, could you repeat that?

*Note: In formal usage, the speaker would follow a sequence of past verb forms: "Did you say your name *was* Yoko?" and "Excuse me, what did you say your name *was*?"

There are four basic types of responses to become familiar with in the above example: (a) a confirming repetition (1 and 2); (b) a questioning repetition (3 and 4); (c) an incomplete repetition with an expectant tone at the end, often with a rise in intonation to indicate a question (5); and (d) ways of requesting a repetition (6 to 10).

Following are more examples. With other students, practice these examples as real-life exchanges. How good an actor are you? For the last three examples, choose your own responses.

Statement	Confirming Repetition	Questioning Repetition	Incomplete Repetition	Request for Repetition
1. I'll meet you at 7:30.	7:30. Okay.	7:30?	You'll meet me at . . .	I'm sorry, what time did you say?
2. The next meeting is on May 8.	May 8. All right.	May 8, did you say?	The next meeting's on . . . ?	I'm sorry, when is the next meeting?
3. That watch costs $39.95.	$39.95, you said.	$39.95, you said?	It costs . . .	*Excuse me, how much did you say it costs?
4. The fare is 75 cents.	75 cents.	75?	It's . . . ?	It's how much?
5. My number's 452-2939.	452-2939 Got it.	452-29 . . . 3 . . . 9?	Your number's 452- . . .	I'm sorry, could you repeat that?
6. My address is 62 Joy St.	62 Joy.	Did you say 62 Joy?	Your address is . . . ?	*Excuse me, what did you say your address is?
7. Turn left at the third traffic light.	Turn left at the third light.	Left at the third light?	Turn left . . .	I'm sorry, I didn't catch that.
8. I'm 18.				
9. I was born in San Juan.				
10. We've been married for two years.				

*Note: In formal usage, the responder would follow a sequence of past verb forms: "Excuse me, how much did you say it *cost*?" and "Excuse me, what did you say your address *was*?"

Exercise 1—Interviews and Introductions

Find out some information from a classmate whom you do not already know. Practice using repetition and request for a repetition to help you. The other student will do the same with you. Write the information below. After you both finish, you will introduce each other to the rest of the class and tell the things that you have learned about each other.

1. What is your name? _____
_____

2. Where are you from? _____
_____

3. How long have you been studying English?
_____
_____

4. Why do you want to improve your ability in English? _____
_____

5. What is your idea of success in life?
_____
_____

6. Any additional information: _____
_____

Exercise 2—Meeting Everyone in Class

Walk around and talk to all of the students in class. Try to find people for whom the following things are true. Add some interesting kinds of information for numbers 15 to 20. When you find a person for whom a piece of information is true, ask that person to sign his or her name on the line next to the information. Be sure to use "you" in your questions and to ask the questions well. Also use repetition or request for a repetition in your conversation whenever you think it will be helpful (whenever you need to hear better or be more sure about either a question or an answer).

Find a person

1. who knows how to work with a computer: _____

2. who sings in the shower or bathtub: _____

3. who has had a pet other than a cat or dog: _____

4. for whom English is a third language: _____

5. who was born in April: _____

6. who does some exercising every day: _____

7. whose parents have different nationalities from each other: _____

8. who enjoys housework: _____

9. who doesn't like to talk on the telephone: _____

10. who hasn't been in a hospital since birth: _____

11. who has read two books in English: _____

12. who plays the guitar: _____

13. who can tell you his or her favorite saying about life: _____

14. who is in love: _____

15. who has never ridden on _____ : _____

16. _____ : _____

17. _____ : _____

18. _____ : _____

19. _____ : _____

20. _____ : _____

Exercise 3—Alternative Identities

You will be in a group with one-half of the students in your class, and the rest of the students will be in a second group. Your group may be first or second to choose well-known names from the list below for the students in the other group. You will not tell your choices. Instead, you will write the names on pieces of paper that you will tape to the backs of the other students. Those students will then try to learn their "identities" by asking *yes/no* questions, questions for which the only answer is "yes" or "no."

The student who guesses his or her "identity" first is the winner. Continue to play until everyone in the group guesses correctly. Then the two groups will reverse responsibilities and play again. Throughout the exercise, including its variations below, use repetition or request for a repetition whenever you think it will be helpful (whenever you need to hear better or be more sure about either a question or an answer).

Note: Before you begin the exercise, your whole class may wish to quickly cross off from consideration any names that are not readily known by everyone. You also may wish to consider names that are not listed. Once the exercise begins, no one should look back at the list.

Variations

1. Pick your own "alternative identity" so that the rest of the class has to ask questions in order to guess it.

2. Play the game with *Wh* questions, questions that cannot be answered with "yes" or "no." The only *Wh* question that cannot be asked is, "Who am I?" (or "Who are you?" under variation 1).

3. Cut out of some magazines the pictures of persons or things, specific or general, that can be identified by everyone, but do not let anyone see them. Tape them to people's backs and play the game as originally described above.

Princess Diana
Prince Charles
Pope John Paul II
Shakespeare
Superman
Cleopatra
Karl Marx
Jane Fonda
Leonardo da Vinci
James Bond
Ronald Reagan
Mickey Mouse
Pele
Larry Bird
Frankenstein
Gandhi
Sherlock Holmes
Mikhail Gorbachev

Beethoven
Margaret Thatcher
Martin Luther
  King, Jr.
John Lennon
  (Beatles)
Christopher
  Columbus
Charles Darwin
Adam (the first
  man)
Eve (the first
  woman)
Lenin
Socrates
Kareem Abdul-
  Jabbar
Don Quixote

George Washington
Ernest Hemingway
Confucius
Elvis Presley
Mao Zedong
Michelangelo
Albert Einstein
Queen Elizabeth
Fidel Castro
Mozart
Mona Lisa
Joseph Stalin
Donald Duck
Galileo
Napoleon
Hamlet
Thomas Edison
King Kong

Pablo Picasso
Plato
Count Dracula
Isaac Newton
Magic Johnson
Bruce Springsteen
Homer
Dante
Cervantes
Cinderella
Muhammad Ali
Madonna
Santa Claus

Exercise 4—Drawing from Directions

Listen to the directions on the tape for making a drawing. Try to repeat each direction after you hear it. When you hear each direction a second time, draw a figure according to that direction in the space provided. Below left are the kinds of figures that you will draw and some of the vocabulary that you will hear. After you finish your complete drawing, the teacher will put the correct picture on the chalkboard. Did you draw it correctly?

Your drawing (begin in the middle of the space):

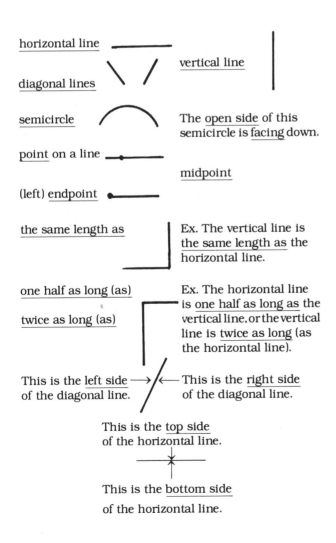

horizontal line

vertical line

diagonal lines

semicircle   The open side of this semicircle is facing down.

point on a line

midpoint

(left) endpoint

the same length as   Ex. The vertical line is the same length as the horizontal line.

one half as long (as)

twice as long (as)   Ex. The horizontal line is one half as long as the vertical line, or the vertical line is twice as long (as the horizontal line).

This is the left side →/← This is the right side
of the diagonal line.   of the diagonal line.

This is the top side
of the horizontal line.

This is the bottom side
of the horizontal line.

Exercise 5—Student Directions for Drawing

Use the figures from exercise 4 to create your own drawing. Then use the vocabulary to give directions to your classmates. Limit yourself to four to five steps. Are your directions clear, direct, and complete? Can the other students follow your directions correctly? The teacher will point out any problems. The whole class should follow these procedures.

1. For one group of direction givers, the listeners may request the repetition of directions. But there may be no more than two requests from the listeners as a group for each direction.

2. For the second group of direction givers, the listeners may repeat the directions aloud. The direction giver will state if a repetition is correct, or he or she will correct it. There may be no more than two repetitions from the listeners as a group for each direction.

3. For the last group of direction givers, the listeners may only listen, repeat the directions silently to themselves, and draw.

Compare the effects of these procedures on both the direction givers and the listeners. Also, compare any effects on the correctness of the drawings.

Exercise 6—Getting Information, I

Your teacher will assign you and a classmate one or more of the following tasks for getting information. In the first conversation, one of you will seek information, and the other will provide it. Then you will reverse roles for a second conversation. Practice using repetition and request for a repetition in each conversation. After you finish your two conversations with your classmate, your teacher may ask you to perform one or both of them in front of the class.

Get information about the following:

1. The names, ages, and occupations of the other person's immediate family members

2. The other person's home town and its special features

3. The other person's favorite pastime—what it is, when it became the person's favorite, and how much time and energy the person now devotes to it

4. When and how the other person met his or her spouse (husband or wife), dating companion, or best friend

5. The other person's current home—the address, the type of place (room, apartment, or house), and any special features of the place

6. The other person's telephone—the number, any problems with service, and any problems with long-distance bills

7. The other person's favorite movie—what it is, who was involved in making it, when and where it was made, what it is about, and why it is the person's favorite

8. The other person's favorite piece of literature—what it is, who wrote it, what it is about, and why it is the person's favorite

9. The other person's favorite TV show—what it is, what it is about, and why it is the person's favorite

10. The other person's favorite form of music, piece of music, musical composer, or musical performer (individual or group)

11. The other person's best vacation—what it was, when it was, and why it was the best

12. The other person's occupational plans—what they are, why the person has formed those particular plans, and what he or she will have to do in order to achieve them

Exercise 7—Getting Information, II

These instructions are the same as for exercise 6, except that instead of dealing with completely factual information, you and your classmate will have the fun of playing roles and using your imaginations in order to provide information.

Get information from the following:

1. A car dealer about the special features of a new car and the cost of the car

2. A movie theater employee about the movie currently playing, the time of its next showing, and the price for a ticket to see it

3. A "special informant" about the telephone number of some famous person and the best time to call the person

4. A famous person about the best time and place for you to meet so that you can interview him or her for your English class

5. A travel agent about departure and arrival times, stops, and ticket prices for traveling by plane to a place of your choice

6. Same as number 5, except substitute train for plane

7. Same as number 5, except substitute bus for plane

8. Same as number 5, except substitute ship for plane

9. A ticket agent about the prices of tickets and the next available date and time for attending a concert, play, opera, ballet, sporting event, or other kind of entertainment

10. A financial adviser about the best current investments for your money

11. An advertiser about the place to live that he or she has advertised for rent

12. A public transportation employee about the routes available and the fares charged by public transportation (bus, subway, or other type) for traveling to a place of your choice in your local area

Exercise 8—Discussion: Success

In *The Case of the Treasure Hunt, or "The Secret to Success,"* it was difficult to know for sure what the treasure was or what Farnsworth and Holmes's idea of success was. Success is, after all, an abstract idea—people have many different thoughts about it. Read the following discussion questions about success and choose one or more to talk about. Before you begin discussing them, however, study the phrases and questions (listed below) used for expressing and asking for an opinion; they can help you participate well in the discussion. Practice using these phrases and questions and learn them.

Discussion Questions

1. Is success a private matter, a social matter, or both?

2. Are there national or cultural definitions of success? Explain with reference to your native culture.

3. Are there different kinds of success for men and women? Explain.

4. In your opinion, what is a successful life?

5. In your opinion, what is an unsuccessful life?

6. How does your idea of success relate to the way you live?

Expressing and Asking for an Opinion in Discussions

Here are some useful phrases and expressions to use to introduce your ideas and to help other people express their ideas.

Expressing an Opinion

1. In my opinion . . .

2. I think (that) . . .
   I feel (that) . . .
   I believe (that) . . .

3. As I see it . . .

4. As far as I'm concerned . . .

5. If you ask me . . .

6. I'd like to say (that) . . .

7. I'd like to point out (that) . . .

Asking for an Opinion

1. What do you think?

2. What's your opinion?

3. How do you feel about it?

4. How do you see it?

5. What's your view (on the matter)?

6. Do you agree (or disagree)?

2 The Case of Hitting Rockbottom

Prelistening: The Situation

John D. Rockbottom is famous for three things. He is the world's richest man, he has absolutely no sense of humor, and he suffers terribly from hydrophobia, the fear of water. And today, April 1—April Fools' Day—he may be the angriest man in the world because of the practical joke that someone has played on him. When he walked into his office in Rockbottom Mansion at 3:00 this afternoon, a balloon full of water fell from the top of the door. It hit him on the head, broke, and covered him with water!

By 4:00, Mr. Rockbottom has brought in private detective Sherlock Holmes and his friend Dr. Watson, and also Inspector Lestrade of Scotland Yard (the police in London), to work on this case. He has also offered a reward of $10,000 to *anyone* who can identify the practical joker.

Instructions

Everyone in class will have a role to play in this mystery. The three students who play Holmes, Watson, and Lestrade will question the suspects. Like most good investigators, they will *repeat* the information that they hear and write notes about it—on the investigative chart below. The other characters will also repeat the information (to themselves) and fill in the chart in hopes of solving the case and collecting the $10,000 reward. Below is an example of how the investigators will proceed. Perform this questioning in class.

Holmes: Who are you?

Suspect: The upstairs maid.

Holmes: The upstairs maid?

Suspect: Yes, that's right.

Holmes: What have you been doing?

Suspect: I've been dusting rooms.

Holmes: Dusting rooms?

Suspect: Yes, uh-huh.

Holmes: How long have you been dusting?

Suspect: I've been dusting for about three hours.

Holmes: Three hours. All right. And how many rooms have you dusted?

Suspect: I've dusted twelve so far.

Holmes: Twelve. All right, thank you. That's all for now.

The teacher will assign you a number. Turn to it in the Roles and Clues section beginning on page 176 to find your role. Play your role exactly as it is described. Also, listen carefully to all of the suspects. One of them (or you) will be the practical joker. You will have a chance to guess who the joker is from the information that he or she gives (or that you give). *Wait until everyone has finished talking so that you can be sure about your guess and collect the $10,000 reward!* If it seems to you that you yourself are the joker, don't show your guilt—try to escape detection!

Use this chart to take notes about the case. Focus your listening on the four areas that head the chart: (1) the *suspects* in the case, (2) the *activities* that they have been performing, (3) the *length of time* that they have been performing them, and (4) the *results* of their activities (how much they have done). Some information has already been noted for you. Add to the chart as you listen to the information and repeat it.

Investigative Chart

Suspect	Activity	Length of Time	Results
Freddie R. – son	playing video games		
Abigail R. – wife			14 letters
cook		2 hours	

Questions

Answer these questions orally or in writing.

1. What kinds of questions do Holmes and the other investigators ask?

2. Why do you think they ask these questions?

3. Why do they repeat the answers that they receive?

4. How many suspects are there in the case?

5. Who are the suspects?

6. What have the suspects been doing, for how long, and how much have they done?

7. Who do you think is the guilty person? Why?

Listening Skill: Repetition, continued

As the preceding chapter explained, repeating information can help you make sure that you have heard something correctly. This can be an important part of conversation. At the same time, there may be situations in which your use of repetition is limited, especially your use of it aloud. In this chapter and the next one, you will have more opportunity to use this listening skill, but limitations will appear. As you proceed, work at internalizing the skill. In other words, practice repeating silently to yourself. Your development of the skill will then become useful in many more situations.

Exercise 1—Interview about Fun Activities

Several of the characters in *The Case of Hitting Rockbottom* were engaged in activities that they cared about to some degree. Find out more about one of your classmates by interviewing the person about the activities he or she cares about— what the person likes (enjoys), loves, or tries to do whenever he or she can. Use *repetition* or *request for a repetition* whenever it is necessary or helpful. Then reverse roles so that your classmate can interview you. Let your entire conversation proceed as naturally as possible. After you finish, share with the rest of the class some of the interesting things that you have learned about each other. Note your interviewee's activities on the numbered lines below.

Example:
A. What do you *like* to do for fun?

B. I like to play video games.

A. Video games?

B. Uh-huh.

A. Me, too. Pac-Man is still my favorite.

B. It's the favorite of a lot of people. Space Invaders is still number one with me, though.

A. Which one did you say? . . .

1. (likes or enjoys) _____

2. (loves) _____

3. (tries to do whenever he or she can) ____
_____

Exercise 2—Interview about Not-So-Fun Activities

A lot of activities in *The Case of Hitting Rockbottom* could not be considered fun activities. Interview your classmate again to find out about the activities he or she does not care for—what the person dislikes, hates (can't stand), or avoids doing whenever possible. Once again, use repetition or request for a repetition whenever it is necessary or helpful. Then reverse roles so that your classmate can interview you. Let your entire conversation proceed as naturally as possible. After you finish, again share some information with the rest of the class. Record the information you receive in the numbered lines below.

Example:

A. What do you *avoid* doing whenever you can?

B. That's easy—I avoid washing dishes.

A. You avoid washing dishes, really?

B. Oh, yes, I'll do anything to escape that. I especially hate doing forks.

A. You hate what?

B. Cleaning forks. I hate having to get in between the prongs. I always end up jabbing myself. . . .

1. (dislikes) _____
   _____

2. (hates or can't stand) _____
   _____

3. (avoids whenever he or she can) _____
   _____

Exercise 3—Drawing a Scene from Directions

Listen to the directions that the teacher gives you for drawing, in the space below, the scene of the Rockbottom case—the Rockbottom estate. The class as a whole may make only one request for a repetition and one repetition aloud for each direction.

Do not spend a lot of time trying to draw a beautiful picture. A correct drawing, not a beautiful one, is the goal.

Your drawing:

Exercise 4—Student Directions for Drawing Scenes

In a group of three or four students, prepare a set of directions for drawing a scene and give them to the rest of the class. Limit yourselves to five to seven directions. You will also follow the other groups' directions for drawing scenes. Listeners as a whole may make only one request for a repetition or one repetition for each direction.

1. _____
    _____
2. _____
    _____
3. _____
    _____
4. _____
    _____
5. _____
    _____
6. _____
    _____
7. _____
    _____

Exercise 5—Jokes

A practical joke, like the balloon full of water in *The Case of Hitting Rockbottom*, is a trick played upon someone. Most jokes, however, are verbal instead of physical, and they are usually told for the amusement of everyone who hears them. Sometimes, though, the jokes "go over people's heads" (people do not understand the jokes) because the jokes contain a trick in language or idea. This happens especially if the joke is very cultural in nature and the listener is from a different culture.

Listen to the following "chicken jokes" on the tape, fill in the missing words in the spaces provided, and decide if you find any humor in the jokes. Make any use of repetition silently, to yourself.

1. The first joke is very old, very well known, and not very clever:

    A. Why did the _____
cross the road?

    B. I _____ —why did the
chicken _____?

    A. To get to the _____!

2. The second joke changes the first joke and plays with two words that sound the same but that have different meanings—*foul*, meaning "bad" or "awful" and *fowl*, meaning "a bird raised for eating, especially a chicken":

    A. _____ the chicken
_____?

    B. I _____ —why?

    A. For some _____.

3. The third chicken joke is completely different:

    A. I had to take my _____ to
the _____ because he thought he
was a _____.

    B. Did the doctor _____?

    A. No, he _____.

    B. That's _____.

    A. Well, not completely. At least we
don't have to _____ anymore.

Compare your responses to these jokes and your opinions of them with the responses and opinions of other students.

Exercise 6—Telling Jokes

Do you have any jokes in your native culture like the ones in exercise 5? Try telling at least one of your favorite jokes in class—in English. Does it translate into English very well? Do your listeners "get it" (understand it), or does it "go over their heads"? If they understand it, do they find it funny or not? Explain the meaning if necessary and discuss the cultural content of the joke—does it belong very much to your native culture or not?

Exercise 7—Discussion: Humor

Humor and laughter differ from person to person, from place to place, from culture to culture, and from time to time. Read the following discussion questions and choose one or more to talk about. First, though, test your memory of the phrases and questions used for expressing and asking for an opinion in a discussion. Write them in the review section on the next page. Review these phrases and questions in order to help yourself participate well in the discussion activity.

Discussion Questions

1. Do you think that the practical joke that was played on Rockbottom was funny or not? Explain.

2. What kinds of things make you laugh?

3. What kinds of humor are popular in your native culture today?

4. To your knowledge, have the kinds of humor changed a lot in your native culture over the years? Explain.

5. Do you believe that some things are universally funny? Explain.

6. Do you agree or disagree with the idea that humor is a means of dealing with anxiety, including anxiety over socially unacceptable desires? Explain.

7. Is it important to have a sense of humor? Explain.

8. Is it important to be able to laugh at yourself? Explain.

Review: Expressing and Asking for an Opinion in Discussions

How many phrases and questions used for expressing and asking for an opinion can you remember? Only after you have checked your memory completely should you refer to the information at the end of chapter 1.

Expressing an Opinion	Asking for an Opinion
1. _____	1. _____
2. _____	2. _____
3. _____	3. _____
4. _____	4. _____
5. _____	5. _____
6. _____	6. _____
7. _____	

Exercise 8—Presentations: Entertainment

Are playing video games, mentioned in *The Case of Hitting Rockbottom* and in exercise 1, your favorite form of entertainment, or do you prefer something else? Maybe you prefer a sport, a kind of music, a kind of reading, certain kinds of television programs, a form of dance, or something else? Make a three- to five-minute presentation about your favorite form of entertainment. You might tell the class why you like it or why you liked one particular experience of it. Study the information below about planning and organizing; it will help you to prepare for and give your presentation.

Planning and Organizing a Presentation

Prepare your presentation by *carefully planning and organizing* it. Here are some useful suggestions:

1. Think carefully about what you want to say.

2. Do not write out your complete presentation for reading to your audience. If you want, you may use an outline written on a sheet of paper or on note cards to help you remember things about your subject.

3. Use a clear organization format that will help you to remember the parts of your presentation and that will help your audience to listen and understand. A very common and useful organization format is the following:

Three major parts

a. *Introduction*
State your main idea and your supporting ideas (your subject and its parts).

Examples

There are three things that make listening to traditional folk music my favorite form of entertainment: (1) the sounds of traditional folk instruments, (2) the ideas about life that are expressed in the songs, and (3) the sense of connection that I feel with everyday people from the past to the present.

b. *Body*
Tell more about your supporting ideas (the parts of your subject), give details about those ideas, and use signal words to help your audience listen and understand.

First of all, the sounds from old instruments, like a dulcimer, a lute, or even a hurdy-gurdy, seem new, fresh, and clean to me. They seem to come straight from the musician, not from an electrical outlet. They also have an intimate sound, drawing me close to the musician and the music . . . *Second, third, fourth, next*, etc. *Last, finally*, etc.

c. *Conclusion*
Briefly summarize or round off your information. Avoid saying something like "That's all." Use appropriate signal words.

The sounds, the ideas, and the oneness with other people *thus* mean a lot to me. I find and support traditional folk music whenever I can, and it in turn gives a special kind of support to me. *In summary, in conclusion*, etc.

3 The Case of the Missing Bracelet

Prelistening: The Situation

In this case, Inspector Lestrade of Scotland Yard comes to Sherlock Holmes with a problem. The problem is this: the man who stole a very valuable bracelet, and who apparently hid the bracelet for safekeeping before his arrest, has just died in prison. Even though he knew he was dying, he refused to reveal where the bracelet was. However, there is information—in particular, a note written in a secret code—that may lead to finding the bracelet. The inspector wants Holmes's help in reclaiming the bracelet from the dead convict.

Instructions

1. Listen to the taped account of the case in order to get a general understanding of it. Then listen again, read the tapescript on the next page as you listen, and fill in the blank spaces. This will help you to focus on important background information and especially on important details regarding the bracelet's whereabouts. At this point, can you determine where the bracelet is? (If you think you have the solution at any time before other students do, do not reveal it—instead, let them have the pleasure of solving the mystery also.)

2. After you have had some time to think alone, your teacher will ask you to discuss the information in the case with a small group of your classmates. Can your group arrive at a solution? (Remember to let students outside your group have the pleasure of solving the mystery on their own.)

3. After you have had some time for group discussion, your teacher will assign you and each of the other students in class an individual number for locating a clue to the mystery in the Roles and Clues section beginning on page 176. Your teacher may even assign you more than one number, depending on the size of the class. In your group, discuss the new information that all of you have received. Can your group solve the mystery now?

4. If you still need more information, then "negotiate" with one or more of the other groups for the information they have. Maybe those students will tell you a new clue if you tell them one—that is one possibility. Get as much information as you need from the other groups in order to solve the case.

Tapescript

Lestrade: It's the end of a bad business, Mr. Holmes. It's over with. Convict Henry Pettibone _____ this morning in his _____ in the infirmary at Dartmoor Prison. The _____ of death has not been determined, but we suspect _____ or some other disease of the intestinal area.

Holmes: Hmm, Henry Pettibone... Inspector Lestrade, isn't Pettibone the _____ who stole the famous Tut gold _____, the one that King Tutankhamen of _____ gave to his wife over _____ years ago?

Lestrade: Yes, of course, Pettibone's the one. And the bracelet's the one that was _____ by Sir Ralph Teasdale during a scientific _____ at one of the _____ in Egypt. Sir Ralph _____ the bracelet to his _____, Lady Diana Teasdale.

Holmes: And of course it was Pettibone who _____ the bracelet from Lady Teasdale while she was _____ at the Copley Hotel.

Lestrade: But it didn't do him any _____ if you remember, Mr. Holmes. We _____ him shortly afterward as he was trying to make his _____ from the hotel.

Holmes: Unfortunately, though, the bracelet _____ after it was stolen. Pettibone didn't _____ it on him when you arrested him. But I don't understand _____ Pettibone didn't try to _____ with someone about the bracelet if he knew he was _____.

Lestrade: But he _____, Mr. Holmes. That's why I've come to _____ you. After three years in _____, he finally wrote this _____ to his _____, but he was unable to _____ it before he died. It's in a secret _____, and we can't figure it out.

Holmes: I don't have my _____. Please read it to me.

Lestrade: It goes like this: _____ _____.

Holmes: All right, let me make sure that I wrote that down correctly. That's _____ _____. Very good, now let's have a _____ at it!

Questions

Answer these questions orally or in writing.

1. Who was Henry Pettibone?

2. Where did he die?

3. What was the cause of his death?

4. Who originally found the Tut gold bracelet? When? Where?

5. What did the finder do with the bracelet?

6. Who stole the bracelet? Where?

7. What happened to the bracelet after it was stolen?

8. Why has Inspector Lestrade come to Sherlock Holmes?

9. Why does Holmes repeat the coded message?

10. What are the letters in the coded message?

11. What is the secret message? In other words, where is the bracelet hidden?

12. Explain the behind-the-scenes actions in the case: why did the thief hide the bracelet in that way, and what resulted afterwards?

Listening Skill: Focusing on Important Details and Ideas

Focusing on important details and ideas is another active listening skill that greatly aids comprehension. "Focusing" means that the listener (1) is aware of the listening context, (2) has a purpose in listening, (3) concentrates on achieving that purpose, (4) judges the general parts of the spoken content that are important for the listening purpose, and (5) selects the particular parts of the spoken content that fulfill the listening purpose.

A conversation between a customer who enters a fast-food restaurant and a restaurant employee who serves customers will provide a good example of focusing in listening. Listen to it on the tape:

Employee: Hi, can I help you?
Customer: Hi. Just a minute, let me see what I want to get. Well . . . okay, I think I'll have a cheese-burger and a milk.
Employee: Cheeseburger and milk. Anything else? . . .

In this example, the employee has understood perfectly. She has been a good listener! She is *aware of the context*: a fast-food restaurant in which people are going to give her their orders for the food and drinks they wish to buy. The *purpose* of her listening activity is to hear immediately and exactly what the customers want. On this occasion as on others, she *concentrates* on listening for food and drink words, she *judges* that the customer at first does some unimportant talking or thinking aloud (he says several words that are not important for her to pay a lot of attention to), and she *selects* from all of his words the ones that matter the most. That is to say, out of the 23 words that the customer speaks, the employee picks out and understands the two that really matter—"cheeseburger" and "milk." She then uses the listening skill of *repetition* to make sure that she has understood the customer's order correctly.

This example is a very simple one, but it does show that "listening to" and "understanding" are really a matter of "listening for" something—for the important words, details, and ideas. That is what "focusing" is all about. In listening to the suspects in *The Case of Hitting Rockbottom*, the important information to listen for was the amount of something done within a period of time. In *The Case of the Missing Bracelet*, it was important to focus on (1) details that were missing from the tapescript and that needed to be filled in, (2) other details that you received from classmates, and (3) ideas that were connected with the details and that developed from them. You were made aware of the context or situation from the beginning, you had a specific purpose for your listening, and you carried out that purpose. Thinking was an important part of the entire listening and understanding process.

The exercises that follow will give you more opportunity to improve your ability to *focus on important details and ideas.*

Exercise 1—Listening Situations

The key words or details in the fast-food restaurant conversation above were, as you heard and read, "cheeseburger" and "milk." Listen to the statements made in the following situations, focus on (listen for) the important details, and write those details on the lines provided.

1. A teacher beginning a class session:

_____

2. A bus driver pointing out sights on a sightseeing tour: _____

_____

3. A consumer shopping for a new watch:

_____

4. An airline employee helping a ticket holder at an airport check-in counter: _____

_____

5. A supermarket employee giving directions:

_____

Exercise 2—Directions to Places

In *The Case of the Missing Bracelet,* at the time of the theft, Henry Pettibone might not have had any trouble getting away with the Tut bracelet if he had listened more carefully to the directions that his assistant had given him about how to make his escape. Unfortunately for him, he got lost in the hotel and then he got caught by the police!

Following directions to places was a part of the previous exercise (number 5), and it is a big part of life in general. The fact is that not knowing where to go or how to get someplace is a common problem. Look at the map below and listen to the conversations on the tape. You will hear one person ask another person for directions to a particular place in the city of Waterbury. The *important details* that you will need to

focus on are (1) the words that describe movements and (2) the words that describe the things to see that are connected with the movements.

After listening to each set of directions and referring to the map, answer the corresponding question below.

1. Where is the Trade Center?

   _____

2. Where is the Strand movie theater?

   _____

3. Where is the Stardust Cafe?

   _____

4. Where is the new French bakery?

   _____

5. Where is Contron Computer Corporation?

   _____

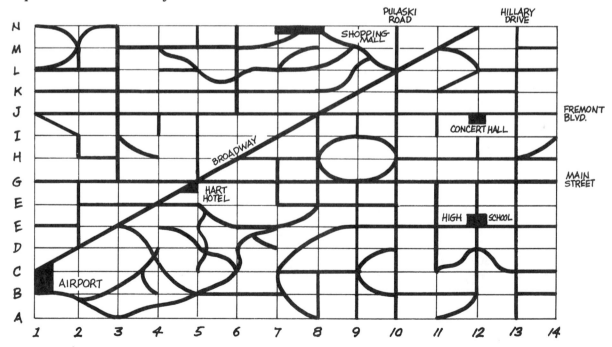

Example: Where is the High School?
             It's at E 12.

Exercise 3—Student Directions

Your teacher will assign you one of the places listed below. Without telling anyone where it is, locate it on the map of Waterbury by letter and number. Give directions to it when the class asks how to get there from one of the other places that has been located on the map.

sports center	city university
library	police station
church	fire department
bus station	telephone company
city hall	radio station
courthouse	zoo
public garden	museum
elementary school	video-games center
playground	train station
hospital	soccer stadium
TV station	performing-arts
post office	center
	bank

The teacher may allow the class to use the skill of repeating aloud in order to find the right locations. People often use that skill when receiving directions to places. In this situation, however, it is especially important to continue working at focusing on important details. Good focusing can reduce the need for repeating or requesting a repetition, which may not always be possible.

Exercise 4—Directions at School

Plan directions to some unrevealed but interesting thing in the school building or on the campus grounds. Give the directions to a classmate and also receive directions from him or her. Follow the directions you receive and return *within ten minutes.* Report what you found, or describe how you got lost!

Exercise 5—News Report

Look at the map below as you listen to the report on the tape about a planned world tour by an American diplomat. Focus your attention on three things: (1) the places that he will visit, (2) the dates of the visits, and (3) the topics of discussion in each place. Use the chart below to record the information that you hear. Some parts have already been completed for you as examples.

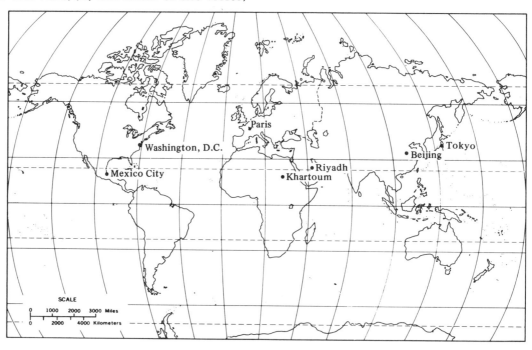

Place	Date	Topic
		Nuclear arms control
Khartoum		
	April 20	

Exercise 6—Movie Critiques

Listen to the critiques, on the tape, of five
new movies. Focus your attention on the
areas that are included in the chart below.
Some parts of the chart already contain
information from the critiques. Add
information to the chart as you listen.

Country	Title	Kind of Movie	Good Points	Bad Points
	Zatoichi vs. Godzilla			Know who will win
France			Good with historical facts	
		Romantic adventure		

Exercise 7—20 Questions

Your teacher will think of a person, place, or thing, but not someone or something famous. You and the rest of the class will then ask questions in order to get information and guess the teacher's word. If you students guess the word in 20 questions or fewer, then you win the game. If you are not able to guess within 20 questions, then the teacher wins. As you play, focus on listening for important details, on repeating those details to yourself if that is helpful, and on actively thinking about the details as you hear them in order to come to a quick solution.

Play the game several times, giving everyone a chance to think of a word that the rest of the class has to guess.

Variation

Think of occupations that others have to guess within 20 questions. The questions that cannot be asked are, "Who are you?" "What are you?" and "What do you do?" To make the game more challenging, you might use only *yes/no* questions.

Exercise 8—Discussion: Politics

Politics is everywhere. Sometimes it is very recognizable, as in the news report exercise in this chapter. At other times it is more subtle, as in the critique of the de Gaulle movie or in the removal of a historical artifact from a country, referred to in *The Case of the Missing Bracelet.* In general, whether we like it or not, politics is very much a part of our lives. Read the following discussion questions about politics and choose one or more to talk about. Before you begin discussing them, however, study the sentences and phrases (next page) used for agreeing and disagreeing; they can help you participate well in the discussion. Practice using these sentences and phrases and learn them.

Discussion Questions

1. What is the number one political priority in the world today? What are the top five priorities?

2. What kinds of responsibilities, if any, do the developed nations have toward the undeveloped nations in the world?

3. How important are talks in solving problems between countries? Is it true that when talking stops, trouble begins? Explain.

4. How effective is the United Nations as a world organization? Should it be changed, perhaps given more power, in order to improve its ability to solve or prevent problems in the world? Explain.

5. Do you agree with the idea that everything in life is ultimately politics? Explain.

6. What is your reaction to the idea that politics is one of the three things in life that are too dangerous to talk about (with religion and sex considered the other two)?

Agreeing and Disagreeing in Discussions

In some of your discussions, you may want to agree or disagree with someone's opinion. It is important to know how to communicate to other people whether or not you share their viewpoints. Here are some sentences and phrases that are useful for communicating that information.

Expressing Agreement

1. I agree (with you).

2. I think you're right.

3. That's a good point.

4. That's what I think.

5. I feel the same way.

6. That's how I see it, too.
That's the way I see it, too.

Expressing Disagreement

1. I disagree (with you).

2. I'm afraid I disagree.

3. I see what you're saying, but . . .

4. Maybe, but . . .

5. I hate to disagree, but . . .

6. That's not completely true. That's not exactly true.

7. (I'm afraid) I can't go along with that.

4 The Case of "Why Is Today a Special Day?"

Prelistening: The Situation

Here is how Sherlock Holmes himself introduces this case: "I have made my fame and fortune primarily by solving extraordinary cases of crime. But some of the most interesting cases I have known are ones that I have only heard about, that involve human interest instead of extraordinary events, and that are handled by the amateur detectives that exist everywhere. Just about all of the people in the world try to solve important cases about life in general almost every day. They do this by focusing on important details and ideas and then adding up those details and ideas into larger meanings. Consider, for example, the Smiths . . . one, two, or three families? . . . and one, two, or three stories, happy or sad?"

Instructions

1. Your class will be divided into three groups.

2. Two groups at a time will leave the classroom, and one group will remain and listen to a speaker on the tape. Each group will listen to a different speaker.

3. After listening to the tape, you should answer the questions in the Listening Stage, below.

4. After all three groups have listened to the tape and have answered the questions in the Listening Stage, you should complete the Discussion Stage by talking together and writing answers to the discussion questions.

Questions

Listening Stage

1. Who was the speaker that your group listened to?

_____

2. Write down the names of the Smith children. Which child is older?

_____

3. Where do the Smiths live?

_____

4. What did the speaker observe?

_____
_____

Discussion Stage

1. Many people in the United States have the name Smith. Did the other groups hear about the same family or different families? Ask the other groups questions to find out.

_____

2. Ask the other groups about the speakers they listened to and what those speakers observed.

_____
_____
_____

3. Why is today a special day?

_____

Listening Skill: Focusing on Important Details and Ideas, continued

It is not practical or necessary, especially when developing listening ability in a second language, to try to hear and understand every word that someone says. In fact, equal concentration on every word can be very demanding, very tiring, and even inappropriate because the individual words that people speak are not equally important in meaning. In other words, we should be more concerned with some information than with other information. We are likely to understand better the important things if we are prepared to listen for them, if we focus our attention on hearing and understanding them.

The last chapter described focusing as a matter of being aware of the listening situation, having a purpose in listening, and making use of concentration, judgment, and selectivity in order to carry out the purpose. In addition to that, when you understand the different kinds of words that speakers use and the different ways that they pronounce them, you can improve your ability to focus on important details and ideas.

The most important or most meaningful words are usually the *content words.* They are nouns, the main parts of action verbs, adjectives, and adverbs. *Function words* like articles, prepositions, linking verbs, helping verbs, and connecting words like *and* have meaning and help to show relationships between content words, but they are relatively less meaningful or less important. As a result, their sounds are often reduced. Content words usually receive clearer pronunciation and more emphasis than function words do. The example of the customer's order in a fast-food restaurant (from the previous chapter) can be used again, this time to show differences in pronunciation and importance among the words. A written form of the spoken order might look like this:

Customer: Hi. J'sta minute, lemme see what I wanna get. Well ... okay, I think I'll hav'a cheeseburger 'n' a milk

The underlined words get more spoken attention, and the circled ones get the most.

Here is another example. The sentence is again written as it might be spoken, and the same underlining and circling are used to show greater spoken attention.

I'm gonna study in th' library 'ntil three a'clock, 'n' th'n I hafta see my teacher in 'iz office

(I'm going to study in the library until three o'clock, and then I have to see my teacher in his office.)

Exercise 1—Listening to the News: Economics, I

Read the tapescript below as you listen to the tape of a radio news report. Then listen again and underline the words that receive emphasis because they are important in the speaker's message. Some are underlined for you. (Do not be concerned with the circlings at this time.)

Compare your results with those of the other students in class. Do you generally agree about which words are emphasized? There may be some disagreement, but for the most part you should agree.

This is Brian Naylor.
The nation's economy grew at a rate of 6.8 percent last year. That's the biggest increase in the Gross National Product since 1951. And it prompted White House spokesman Larry Speakes to state, quote, "If this were almost any other country in the world, the economic performance of the United States would be termed a miracle." Commerce Secretary Malcolm Baldrige, while more restrained, was still optimistic:

So, with lower interest rates and inflation under control, the economy is in a good position to achieve the 4 percent growth rate expected by the Administration over the course of 1985. To reinforce the staying power of this expansion in the years ahead, our first priority has got to be a reduction in the federal deficit to help hold down inflation and bring down interest rates further.

In the fourth quarter of last year the GNP grew at a rate of 3.9 percent. That's better than anticipated.

Exercise 2—Listening to the News: Economics, II

Generally, a speaker will emphasize some content words in a sentence even more than others in order to make his or her message clear. Listening for these words in particular is a good way to get at least a general understanding of what you hear, and it is a good way to begin improving listening comprehension.

Return to the tapescript in exercise 1, listen to the tape again, and circle the underlined words that get the most emphasis. Some are already circled for you. Does the class agree about the words that get the most emphasis?

Exercise 3—Listening to the News: Disasters

Follow the same procedures as you did in exercises 1 and 2 for the following two news items. First, simply listen to the tape and read along; then listen and underline the words that receive emphasis; and finally, listen a third time and circle the words that are most emphasized.

1. A U.S. military air transport plane crashed in the Caribbean Sea off the coast of Honduras this morning. Twenty-one U.S. military personnel were on board the craft, said to be on a routine tactical airlift mission. No word on possible survivors. Rescue efforts are being hampered by bad weather.

2. Propeller parts were found as far as a half mile from the scene of yesterday's plane crash in Reno that killed sixty-five people. There were three survivors. The reports could indicate that the four-engine prop-jet airliner lost two propellers before it crashed. According to the *Reno Gazette-Journal*, the plane was also leaking fuel. Federal investigators are still looking for any evidence, including two black-box recorders, that could explain the crash.

Exercise 4—Listening to the News: Weather and Its Effects

This tme the tapescript below will contain only the words that receive emphasis. As you listen to the tape, circle the words that receive the most emphasis. Do *not* fill in any blanks. Then answer the questions that follow.

_____ Florida's northern panhandle _____ Miami Beach, Arctic air _____ covering _____ state, _____ many cities registering _____ lowest temperatures _____ record. _____ called _____ freeze _____ century. _____ past two nights _____ subfreezing temperatures _____ severely affected Florida's agricultural industry. NPR's Jo Miglino reports:

_____ 75 percent _____ Florida's citrus crops _____ trees, state agriculture officials say _____ weeks _____ damage done _____ freeze _____ assessed. _____ today inspectors visited groves _____ begin _____ task. There _____ found oranges _____ frozen _____ solid balls _____ ice. _____ cold-damaged fruit _____ still _____ used _____ juice. _____ tomorrow_____ expected _____ state's Citrus Commission _____ call _____ temporary embargo _____ fresh-fruit shipments _____ state _____ prevent poor quality fruit _____ sold.

Citrus _____ not _____ only crop _____ damaged _____ freeze. Florida's winter vegetables _____ also severely affected. State agriculture officials called _____ pepper, squash, _____ cucumber crops total losses.

_____ two nights _____ trying _____ save _____ harvests, Florida farmers _____ get little rest tonight. Another hard freeze _____ expected _____ another cold front _____ predicted _____ cover _____ state _____ weekend.

_____ Jo Miglino, National Public Radio, reporting.

Questions

1. How low are the temperatures in Florida?

_____

2. How can the frozen oranges be used?

_____

3. What has been damaged besides citrus crops?

_____

4. What is the weather going to be like in Florida over the next few days?

_____

Exercise 5—Listening to a News Feature: Interview Format

This time the tapescript will contain only the words that receive the most emphasis. Listen to the tape carefully, follow the tapescript below, but do *not* mark it in any way. Then answer the questions that follow:

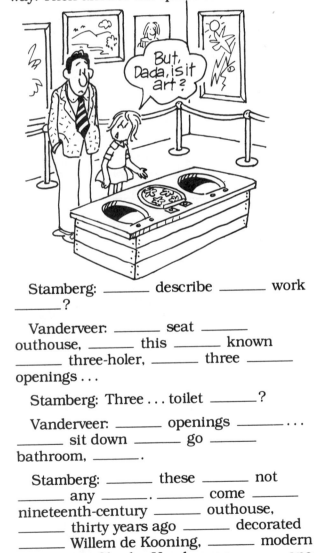

Stamberg: _____ describe _____ work _____?

Vanderveer: _____ seat _____ outhouse, _____ this _____ known _____ three-holer, _____ three _____ openings . . .

Stamberg: Three . . . toilet _____?

Vanderveer: _____ openings _____ . . . _____ sit down _____ go _____ bathroom, _____.

Stamberg: _____ these _____ not _____ any _____. _____ come _____ nineteenth-century _____ outhouse, _____ thirty years ago _____ decorated _____ Willem de Kooning, _____ modern art master. Charles Vanderveer _____ one-third owner _____ "throne," _____ certain _____ unsigned work _____ de Kooning's.

Vanderveer: Two _____ covers _____ missing. One _____ original cover. _____ painted _____— _____ by him— _____. _____ Mrs. de Kooning verified _____ painted _____. _____ didn't paint _____ thing _____ idea _____ major piece _____ art _____. _____ not _____ saying. _____— _____ look _____, _____ style _____ period. _____ painter _____— _____ mind _____ style _____ painting _____— _____ this _____ decorate _____ building.

Stamberg: _____ color _____ . . .

Vanderveer: White . . .

Stamberg: . . . _____?

Vanderveer: _____ seat _____ painted _____ white, _____ medium _____ white _____, _____ before _____ dry, _____ went over _____ another color. _____ blacks _____ blues _____.

Stamberg: _____ anybody _____ know _____ a de Kooning? _____ maybe _____ think _____ a Jackson Pollock? _____ . . .

Vanderveer: _____ evidence _____ Pollock _____, too.

Stamberg: _____ yeah?!

Vanderveer: Pollock's book _____ life— _____— _____ mentions _____ went there _____ 1954— _____ there— _____ house _____ rented _____ Franz Kline, Willem de Kooning . . . De Kooning _____ recognized _____ Pollock being there _____. _____ de Kooning doesn't remember painting _____.

Stamberg: _____ this thing _____ auction? _____ right?

Vanderveer: I _____ commissioned _____ sell _____ contents _____ house. _____ particular object, _____, "_____ sell _____ too." _____ took _____, _____ owners told _____ painted _____ de Kooning. _____ auction, _____ mentioned this, _____— people laughed _____.

Stamberg: _____.

Vanderveer: _____ time _____ sell _____, _____ didn't go _____, _____ I bought _____ fifty dollars. _____, _____ went up _____ owners _____, _____, "_____ I bought _____ seat _____, _____ authenticated, _____ you _____ part _____ whole thing." _____ did get _____ authenticated _____ giving away one-third _____, _____ I _____ talked _____ other people, _____ maintained _____ other third.

Stamberg: _____ original _____ work _____ major American artist. _____ what— _____ sale?

Vanderveer: _____ unusual _____. _____ not _____ painting _____ canvas _____. _____ offered _____ sale _____ Sotheby's _____ Christie's, _____ wrote back _____ didn't think _____ thing _____ . . .

Stamberg: _____! . . .

Vanderveer: . . . sold _____ public auction.

Stamberg: _____! . . .

Vanderveer: _____ that— _____ get away _____ that statement, _____ sell anything _____ public auction. Now, _____, _____ next thing _____ get _____ art world involved _____, _____ somebody _____ what _____ feel _____.

Stamberg: _____ pick up _____ something _____.

Vanderveer: _____ worth _____ money.

Stamberg: _____.

Vanderveer: _____ more _____ fifty dollars.

Stamberg: _____, indeed. _____ last de Kooning _____ two million. Charles Vanderveer _____ auctioneer _____ Bridgehampton, _____.

Questions

1. What object are the two speakers discussing? What is unusual about it?

_____

_____

2. Who painted the object?

_____

3. What has resulted from efforts to sell the object at public auction?

_____

_____

4. Do the speakers think that someone will pay a lot of money for the object? Why or why not?

_____

_____

Exercise 6—Listening to a Commentary

You will hear a woman discuss rules for living with a retired husband. This subject is of interest because traditionally in the United States married people, especially men, have trouble leaving their life of work and adjusting to a full-time life at home with their spouses. This situation can occur at many different ages since there is no standard retirement age in the United States. Some places of employment may require retirement at a certain age, often seventy. However, many Americans now want to continue working past seventy. Others retire at sixty-five. Still others have had the kind of work or have made the kinds of plans that make it possible for them to retire earlier—in their fifties or, in some cases, even in their forties.

Listen to what the woman on the tape says about her situation with her husband and mark each statement below true or false.

	T	F
1. Kim's husband has been retired for only a short time.	____	____
2. One of her rules is that a wife should not have lunch with her retired husband.	____	____
3. Mel retired at an early age.	____	____
4. She recommends spending as much time as possible with a retired husband.	____	____
5. She really doesn't like her husband's using the kitchen, but she respects his right to use it.	____	____
6. She believes that retired people have a right to privacy from each other.	____	____
7. Retired people often remember things differently, according to her.	____	____
8. The five rules that she gives are complete—no more are necessary.	____	____
9. She treats her subject both humorously and seriously.	____	____
10. She and her husband are thinking about getting divorced.	____	____

Exercise 7—Listening to an Extended News Report

You will hear a report about how the U.S. government has refused to accept decisions by an international court, both at the present time and especially at the beginning of this century. No mention is made that other countries, like France, Turkey, Iceland, and Iran, have made similar refusals, and no explanations are given for the U.S.'s refusals.

After you finish listening to the tape, check off all the information that you heard about the formation of the Central American Court of Justice:

_____ It was formed in 1907.

_____ There was a lot of fighting in Central America at the time.

_____ The U.S. had a leading role in the formation of the court.

_____ The U.S. acted out of self-interest in the formation of the court.

_____ The meetings and conventions that were held, starting in 1907, and that involved the U.S., Mexico, and the Central American nations had other positive results besides the formation of the court.

_____ The hope among some people at the time was that courts like this would use international law to prevent wars.

_____ There was opposition in the U.S. to the government's involving itself in the formation of the court.

Now fill in the blanks in the following paragraphs with your own choice of words (this is not a tapescript):

In its early successful years of operation, the court stopped a war between

_____ .

It even had representatives in the Central American countries to make sure

_____ .

Billionaire Andrew Carnegie donated $100,000 to _____

_____ .

The court was first weakened in 1912 when the U.S. _____

_____ .

Then, in 1916, after the U.S. had signed a treaty with the government it supported in Nicaragua, giving the U.S. the right to

_____ ,

the other Central American nations _____

_____

_____ .

The Central American Court ruled _____

_____

the U.S., but the U.S. _____ .
As a result, the Central American Court

_____ .

The commentators appear to be sympathetic toward _____
_____ because _____

_____ .

Exercise 8—Listening to Today's News

Listen to the news on television or radio and note, on the lines below, three stories for reporting on in class. What reactions do you and the other students have to these stories?

1. _____
   _____
   _____

2. _____
   _____
   _____

3. _____
   _____
   _____

Exercise 9—Discussion: News Reporting

One reply to the question, "What's new?" (what has happened or is happening) is, "The news." The news happens every day, every minute, every second. Read the following discussion questions about the news and choose one or more to talk about. First, though, test your memory of the sentences and phrases used for expressing agreement and disagreement in a discussion. Write them in the review section on the next page. Review these sentences and phrases in order to help yourself participate well in the discussion activity.

Discussion Questions

1. Are you satisfied with the news coverage you see or hear in the United States or in your native country? Why or why not?

2. *What to report* and *in how much detail* are constant concerns in news reporting. Because of that, do you think it is possible to satisfy all the people who follow the news? Explain.

3. Should the people who report the news report information that may be critical of their country's government? Explain.

4. It is often said that news professionals have a "responsibility to inform the public." How do you define that responsibility?

5. Do news professionals have a responsibility to look at all sides of an issue, for example an issue between countries? Explain.

6. What part, if any, does entertainment have in news reporting? What part does making money have? Or even, what part does controlling public opinion have?

7. Do you think there is something in human nature that makes us like to hear about deaths, disasters, crimes, scandals, and other negative things? Explain.

8. If you were the producer of a nightly thirty-minute news show, on TV or radio, how would you organize your show? Give the reasons for the organization that you would develop.

Review: Agreeing and Disagreeing in Discussions

How many sentences and phrases used for expressing agreement or disagreement can you remember? Only after you have checked your memory completely should you refer to the information at the end of chapter 3.

Expressing Agreement	Expressing Disagreement
1. _____	1. _____
2. _____	2. _____
3. _____	3. _____
4. _____	4. _____
5. _____	5. _____
6. _____	6. _____
	7. _____

Exercise 10—Presentations: News

The news reporting in exercises 1 through 7, above, is from "All Things Considered" (ATC), a nightly one-and-a-half hour news program on National Public Radio in the U.S. ATC follows a news-magazine format, reporting on current events but also presenting features of interest. Many people like the show for one or more of the following reasons: (1) Unlike the commercially supported TV and radio news programs in the U.S. that concentrate on politics and problems of various kinds, ATC offers a better balance of information by considering many subjects and by reporting on positive as well as negative happenings; (2) ATC usually reports in depth on current events and other matters of interest; (3) ATC is not reluctant to appear critical of the U.S. government, as in exercise 7, above, or of other organizations or individuals in the public eye.

All news reporting is selective, and many people feel that the selections, even on ATC, are too much concerned with politics and negative happenings. Positive matters, like achievements in the arts, the sciences, and other areas, get comparatively little attention.

Prepare and present the kind of news item *that you would like to hear.* It can be of the current-event type, as in exercises 1–4, above, or more like a feature, as in exercises 5–7. It can be something that you know about that has not been widely reported, or it can be something that you imagine. It can be about someone or something far from your class or even in your class, but it has to be of interest to many people. It should be from one to three minutes long. Study the information below about using specific language; it will help you to prepare for your presentation.

Note: Your class may want to organize itself so that the news presentations form one or more complete news shows. You may even want to choose a name for your show.

Specific Language in Presentations

For all presentations, a presenter should try to use the most specific language possible. This may be especially important in news reporting since the audience wants to know the "hard facts" about *who, what, where, when, how,* and *why.* For example, compare the following two statements:

1. A Mexican writer won an important award for his work a few years ago.

2. Gabriel García Márquez, the Colombian-born novelist now living in Mexico, won the 1982 Nobel Prize for Literature for such works as *One Hundred Years of Solitude* and *Chronicle of a Death Foretold.*

The second statement is much more satisfying because it is more specific. Be as specific as possible in your news presentation and in the other presentations that you do.

5 The Case of the Spaceman Spy

Prelistening: The Situation

Sherlock Holmes is once again faced with the responsibility of solving an extraordinary case. However, the case is not "extraordinary" in any ordinary sense of that word. In fact, it is *so* extraordinary that it involves an alien from outer space! Holmes's job is to identify this spaceman spy, who has attempted to steal an important industrial secret on Earth—the formula to Cosmic Cola!

Instructions

1. Listen to the taped account of the case in order to get a general understanding of it. Then listen again, read the tapescript as you listen, and fill in the blank spaces below. The spaces are for important *content words* in the story.

2. After you finish listening and filling in the blanks, answer the questions that follow.

Tapescript

For Sherlock Holmes, it is the case of the century—perhaps the _____ century!

At the World Supermarket Exposition in New York, an industrial spy has attempted to _____ the secret formula to a new space-age _____, Cosmic Cola, a complete _____ in a soda _____. The Exposition has been attended by _____ of people because the products on display include not only the _____ items that are available in supermarkets, but also _____ products that may become available in the future. Among the futuristic products, Cosmic Cola has received the most _____ because it is the most _____ and has the greatest _____-making potential.

The police are holding _____ suspects, all of whom claim to be U.S. _____ and all of whom were in the _____ of the Cosmic Cola display at the _____ of the attempted theft. The police have asked Mr. Holmes for assistance in _____ the suspects because of one very unusual _____ —they believe the spy is from _____ ! Just before the attempted theft, several people reported that they saw a _____ land near the exposition center and that they also saw someone _____ of the UFO before it flew away again.

Holmes: Could you explain, sir, _____ you are and _____ you were doing at the time of the attempted theft?

Suspect number 1: Sure. I'm Fred Taylor from St. Paul, Minnesota, and I'm here in New York on _____. I was trying to get to the _____ farm display because the idea of _____ fish in a supermarket and selling them so _____ really interested me. But the problem was I got _____, and I was walking down the aisle past the Cosmic Cola display when the police _____ me. And that's all.

Holmes: So you're a _____ and you walked down the wrong aisle while you were trying to find the _____. Then the police got you. All right. And how about _____—who are you and what were you doing?

Suspect number 2: I'm Robert Gordon, from Miami, Florida. I'm an _____ salesman, and I'm in New York for a _____ meeting in our national office. I came over to the Exposition during our _____ break, and I thought I'd try a McSushiburger, an _____ product that's a combination of Japanese sushi and American _____. I was just wandering around _____, and I guess I ended up in the _____ place at the _____ time.

Holmes: I see. In other words, you _____ your insurance meeting and came over here to eat _____. You were looking around at things and just _____ to be near the Cosmic Cola display when the _____ started. All right. And how about you?

Suspect number 3: Malcolm Landry, sir, resident of the great state of _____. I work for the _____ of the United States in the field of _____ affairs, and I came down here to New York for the _____ to deliver some papers to the American ambassador to the _____ _____. I was on my way to buy a _____ of eggs, a _____ of milk, and a _____ of bread for dinner when I _____ the eggs, slipped on the broken parts, and _____ into the Cosmic Cola display. I'm a victim of _____, but the police won't believe me.

Holmes: I see. If I understand you correctly, you're a diplomat from Washington "_____." You came "_____" here to New York "just for the _____," and you were buying _____ food for dinner—a "_____" of eggs, a "_____" of milk, and a "_____" of bread—and you had an _____ with the eggs. All right, thank you and thanks also to the other two gentlemen. No more questions. Officer, _____ your spaceman!

Questions

Answer these questions orally or in writing.

1. What kind of exposition is taking place in the story?

2. What crime has been attempted?

3. What is special about Cosmic Cola?

4. How many suspects are there in the case?

5. Where do the police think the guilty person is from? Why?

6. What does Holmes learn from the first suspect?

7. What does he learn from the second suspect?

8. What does he learn from the third suspect?

9. Who is the spaceman spy? How do you know it is he? List all of the reasons for your conclusion.

10. Why does Holmes summarize what he hears from each suspect? How does this help him understand the case and solve the mystery?

Listening Skill: Summarizing

Summarizing what you hear, which is expressing the main idea or ideas in your own words, is often a good listening skill to use, especially in conversation. The information may be important, and summarizing is a way to make sure that you heard it correctly. If you summarize incorrectly, your conversation partner will almost always correct you and help you to understand.

Summarizing is also an aid to thinking, especially in a new language, because you focus on the important parts and on the general meaning of what you hear, not on each individual word. It is also an aid because you put the content into your own words in the new language.

Finally, as with the listening skill of repetition or request for a repetition, summarizing in conversation shows the other person that you have been listening, and better communication will result.

Listen to the example on the tape and fill in the blank spaces below as you listen.

Statement	Possible Summarizing Response
Mr. Brown used to teach at a _____ that had a lot of _____ on campus. He said that sometimes it seemed as if there were more _____ than students. And one beautiful _____ day, when he held a class _____ on the grass, he actually found _____ dogs present and only six _____!	So, for Mr. Brown, there really were more _____ than _____ at his old school that day. That's _____!

There are, of course, many other possible responses. Here is a list of words and phrases often used in summarizing:

1. So . . .
2. In other words . . .
3. It sounds as if . . .
4. It sounds like . . .
5. If I understand you correctly . . .
6. Let me go over that again.
7. Let me see if I have that straight.

Exercise 1—Summarizing People's Statements, I

Listen to the statements on the tape and fill in the blank spaces below. Then summarize the main idea briefly on the lines provided. The first one is done for you as an example.

1. It's amazing how some places get a _**bad**_ reputation: for example, _**New York City**_. There have been so many movies and TV shows showing crime and _**violence**_ there that a lot of people are _**afraid**_ to even visit. But it's really a _**great**_ city and millions of people _**like**_ living and working there. Yes, there are some _**problem**_ areas in New York, but almost _**every**_ big city in the world has _**areas**_ like that.

Summary: So you think many people have gotten a negative view of New York from TV shows and the movies. You feel that the real New York has much more good than bad.

2. My wife and I are very happy about a _____ that we bought in a _____ furniture store. It's a big oak desk, very _____ and very well _____. Like a lot of _____ things, it's much _____ than most of the _____ types that you see nowadays.

Summary: _____
_____
_____
_____

3. Let me give you some advice about how to be _____ in school. First of all, it's important of course to _____ and to get work done on time. But it's also important to find time to study or pursue those _____ that interest _____ personally. And another thing—make sure that you fit in some _____ and relaxation. It's sad to see some people have _____ because all they do is _____ all the time.

Summary: _____
_____
_____
_____

4. There really are different levels of _____. For example, when you're _____, you might think that you understand something well, maybe what it's like to have a _____. And you _____ understand. But, then, when the _____ experience of parenthood comes along, you understand _____ somehow, at a much _____ level.

Summary: _____
_____
_____
_____

5. Memorable meals—most people who _____ have had memorable meals, those _____ experiences they can tell you about, especially from the time they first _____ cooking. As for me, how can I ever forget my first attempt at making _____ , Chinese style, and adding the only other ingredient I could find in the house— _____ ? To this day, at least in my memory, I have never _____ from that once-in-a-lifetime specialty— _____ . Yuck!

Summary: _____
_____
_____
_____

6. I've had a _____ day so far. First, my _____ wouldn't start, so I had to take the _____ to school, and I got here _____ . Then I remembered that I left my _____ at home and that I didn't have enough money to _____ lunch. And now I'm afraid someone has taken my _____ , after I left it by accident in the library. What a day!

Summary: _____
_____
_____
_____

7. Someone should do a study not on the _____ of violence on TV and in the movies, but on the _____ violence is shown. Most of it seems very _____ because people who are punched or shot or crashed into seem to _____ around as if very _____ had happened to them. Other violence is shown in a very _____ way, as if it were a form of _____ to be appreciated. Why can't the _____ about violence be shown?

Summary: _____
_____
_____
_____

Exercise 2—Summarizing People's Statements, II

Listen to the statements on the tape and write only your summaries of them—what you think the main ideas are. The first one is done for you as an example.

1. *In other words you think that simply complaining about the food is really unfair. You think the criticism should be constructive.*

2. _____

3. _____

4. _____

5. _____

6. _____

7. _____

Exercise 3—Student Statements for Summarizing

Use the lines below to plan at least three everyday statements or observations that your classmates can summarize orally, as part of a conversation with you. Summarize orally what your classmates say also. And do not stop your conversation after one summarizing—see how long you can talk with each other naturally.

1. _____

2. _____

3. _____

Exercise 4—Partitives and Groceries

One thing that helped Sherlock Holmes identify the alien in *The Case of the Spaceman Spy* was the alien's poor knowledge of partitives in English. Partitives are comparatively less important than the things they are connected with, so people generally do not focus their listening on them as much. However, a failure to use them correctly will cause listeners to shift their focus onto the failure and away from the speaker's intended emphasis, or intended message.

Work with a group of three or four other students to determine the proper partitives for the items below. There may be more than one possibility in some cases. Fill in the blanks and compare your results with the rest of the class's.

1. a _____ of milk

2. a _____ of light cream

3. a _____ of butter

4. a _____ of butter
(one of the usual four parts in a package)

5. a _____ eggs or a _____ of eggs

6. a _____ of margarine
(round plastic container)

7. a _____ of bread

8. a _____ of bananas

9. a _____ of lettuce

10. a 5 lb. _____ of potatoes

11. a _____ of peas
(round metal container)

12. a _____ of frozen carrots

13. a _____ of cereal

14. a _____ of strawberry jam

15. a _____ of catsup

16. a _____ of soda
(six in number)

17. a _____ of paper towels

18. a _____ of toothpaste

19. a _____ of hand soap

20. a candy _____

Exercise 5—Paying Attention to Function Words: Inserting *A, An, The, Some,* and *Any,* I

Because *content words* usually have the most meaning in a message, we pay especially close attention to them. But *function words* are also important because they have meaning and because they help to connect the content words. They are usually spoken with less emphasis and with reduced pronunciation, but if they are not spoken at all, if they are left out, problems result. The articles *a, an,* and *the* and the related determiners *some* and *any* —all in relation to count and noncount nouns—are a good example. If they are left out or misused, the immediate problem is that the way of speaking sounds odd or nonstandard.

In this exercise, you will hear a story in which these five words have been repeatedly left out. Listen to the tape, follow the tapescript, and insert the appropriate one of the five wherever necessary. Use a caret (ʌ) for your insertions.

Example: I work best in ʌ afternoon.
the

Discuss your insertions and then listen to the story repeated with the five words included in all the proper places.

Mostefa and the Count

Mostefa went to movies last night. He saw new movie, *Count Dracula Bites Dust.* Because movie was very exciting, Mostefa ate three boxes of popcorn and drank four cups of soda. After movie, Mostefa was little sick. He went home and got into bed immediately. He fell asleep in little while, but he had very bad dream—nightmare. He dreamed that Count Dracula was very angry with him because he ate all of popcorn and drank all of soda in theater. He didn't leave popcorn or soda for Count! He dreamed that Count Dracula was very, very hungry! Finally, Mostefa woke up, got out of bed, and went into kitchen. He made popcorn, put it and soda on table for Dracula, and then went back to bed.

Exercise 6—Inserting *A*, *An*, *The*, *Some*, and *Any*, II

The directions here are the same as for exercise 5.

Mostefa, the American Football Kicker?

Mostefa is thinking about trying to become professional football player in United States. He read article in newspaper about many foreign-born soccer players playing American football. It said that these soccer players have very small job. They are on playing field for only few seconds at time to make special kicks. First, they kick football to other team to start first half or second half of game. That is called "kickoff." They also try to kick ball between goal posts at ends of field to score points for their team. If they kick successfully from long distance, it is "field goal"—three points for their team. If they kick successfully from short distance—after their team moves ball into one of two "end zones" for six points, "touchdown"—then they get "extra point" for their team. After extra point or field goal, they also have to "kick off" to other team.

The ten to twenty kickers who are most successful in this work earn hundreds of thousands of dollars year. But it is dangerous job. During few seconds that kicker is on field, there is possibility of violent contact with much bigger and stronger players. Serious injuries may result. Sure, medical bills that also would result would be paid by team owners or by insurance company, but pain would belong entirely to kicker.

Mostefa is going to think some more about all of possibilities before making decision.

Exercise 7—Student Stories

With other students in a small group, write your own very short story about Mostefa. A story that involves partitives in a supermarket, in a restaurant, or at a dinner party might be a good possibility. Tell your story to the other groups in class. They will listen for any problems with determiners (*a*, *an*, *the*, *some*, and *any*) and partitives, and they will summarize your story. You and your group will do the same when you listen to the stories told by the other groups.

Discussion 8—Discussion: Food, Spying, Outer Space, Police

The Case of the Spaceman Spy was a mixture of many things—science-fiction, spying, crime, mystery, and consumerism, to name the most obvious. Read the wide range of discussion questions that have been derived from the story and choose one or more to talk about. Before you begin discussing them, however, study the information below about clarifying; it can help you participate well in the discussion. Practice using these clarifying expressions and learn them.

Discussion Questions

1. What is your opinion of some of the foods and other products that are available in supermarkets today? What would be your opinion of a product like Cosmic Cola?

2. How do you feel about spying and selling a country's secrets? Does *who* commits these acts make a difference? Do these activities help to keep a balance of power in the world and thus provide security?

3. What would you do if you were alone and you met an alien from outer space?

4. Do you see any problem in the fact that billions of dollars are spent on exploring outer space while millions of people on earth suffer from so many problems, including starvation?

5. What is your reaction to militaristic uses of outer space?

6. How much authority should police have in trying to prevent crimes and in responding to them when they happen? What kinds of restraints should be placed on police in order to protect people's rights?

Clarifying in Discussions

Sometimes, during a discussion, one of your statements may not be completely clear to another person or other people. Or maybe another person's statement will not be completely clear to you and others. Here are some useful expressions for trying to clarify (make clear) what you have said or what another person has said. If you do not clarify another person's statement to his or her satisfaction, that person will most likely try to resolve the problem.

Clarifying Your Statement	Clarifying Another Person's Statement
1. I mean . . .	1. You mean . . .
2. In other words . . .	2. In other words . . .
3. What I mean . . .	3. What you mean is . . .
4. What I'm saying is . . .	4. What you're say-ing is . . .
5. What I said was . . .	5. What you said was . . .
6. Let me explain what I mean.	
7. Let me put it another way.	
8. Let me repeat what I said.	
9. Let me rephrase that.	

6 The Case of the Roundabouts

Prelistening: The Situation

While *The Case of the Spaceman Spy* was marked by an extraordinary alien being, *The Case of the Roundabouts* is marked by extraordinarily human characters—Mrs. Gabriela Roundabout and her husband, Brigadier General Slocum Roundabout. They themselves are the complications that turn an ordinary domestic situation into a challenging mystery. Sherlock Holmes must focus on the important details of their characters as well as on the important details of the case. He must then summarize the essential meanings he discovers in order to find Mrs. Roundabout's lost diamond tiara—valued at over $15,000!

Instructions

1. There are ten sections in the taped account of this case. After you hear each section there will be time for you to summarize the information given in that section by Holmes's visitor, Mrs. Roundabout. Write your brief summaries on the lines below. Practice using the common expressions for summarizing discussed in Chapter 5.

Examples:
So you actually like rainy weather.
In other words, you were very sick.
It sounds as if you may change your plans.

(These examples are not related to the story.)

2. After you have been given time for summarizing, you will hear Sherlock Holmes's own summaries. Compare your summarizing with his to see if you agree about the general meaning of each section.

Summaries for the Ten Sections

1. _____
_____

2. _____
_____

3. _____
_____

4. _____
_____

5. _____
_____

6. _____
_____

7. _____
_____

8. _____
_____

9. _____
_____

10. _____
_____

Questions

Answer these questions orally or in writing.

1. How would you describe Mrs. Roundabout?

2. During the General's recent war service, what was he in charge of protecting when he got wounded?

3. Is the General still connected with the army in active service? Explain.

4. Describe the General's overall condition.

5. How did Mrs. Roundabout's diamond tiara become lost? Describe the circumstances.

6. Can you guess with Holmes where the General put the tiara? Consider carefully the General's career and recent experience, the Roundabouts' place of residence, and also the General's "slowing down."

7. Why does Holmes tell Mrs. Roundabout that she may "*explode* with laughter" when he tells her where he thinks the tiara is? What little joke is he making?

8. What does the word "roundabout" mean? Try to guess, or use a dictionary if necessary. Why is that a good name for Mrs. Roundabout and for the General? Why is the title of the case appropriate?

Listening Skill: Summarizing and Paraphrasing

Paraphrasing is closely related to summarizing and is also an active listening skill. It is another way of putting what you hear into your own words. The only difference is that with paraphrasing you may use as many words as the number you hear. With summarizing, you usually use fewer words to express the main idea or ideas of a statement. In *The Case of the Roundabouts*, Sherlock Holmes seemed to both summarize and paraphrase.

Like summarizing, paraphrasing is an aid to thinking in a new language; it helps ensure that you have heard something correctly, and it generally improves communication.

Exercise 1—Paraphrasing "Multisyllabic Verbiage"

Paraphrasing is especially useful when you hear a "plethora of multisyllabic verbiage"— that is, many big words. Listen to the tape. On the lines below, write the "multisyllabic verbiage" that you hear on the left and your paraphrases on the right. The first one is done for you as an example.

1. *educational institution*   1. *School*
2. _____   2. _____
3. _____   3. _____
4. _____   4. _____
5. _____   5. _____
6. _____   6. _____
7. _____   7. _____
8. _____   8. _____
9. _____   9. _____
10. _____   10. _____

Exercise 2—Paraphrasing Euphemisms

Euphemisms are words or phrases that are used in a roundabout or indirect way to refer to things that have few or no positive associations or that make people feel uncomfortable. They attempt to make something sound better than it is or to disguise the hard reality of it. For example, we say "white meat" and "dark meat" when we're eating chicken or turkey because there was a time when people felt uncomfortable saying "breast" and "thigh," words that could refer to parts of humans. Other examples occurred in *The Case of the Roundabouts* with regard to things like war, senility, and the bathroom.

Listen to the tape. On the lines provided, write the euphemisms that you hear on the left, and then try to write your paraphrases on the right. If you are unable to paraphrase some, try working on them in a group. If your group cannot paraphrase some, use a dictionary. The first one is done for you as an example.

1. *pre-owned automobile*
2. _____
3. _____
4. _____
5. _____
6. _____
7. _____
8. _____
9. _____
10. _____

1. *used car*
2. _____
3. _____
4. _____
5. _____
6. _____
7. _____
8. _____
9. _____
10. _____

Exercise 3—Indirect Wording by Students

In this exercise, instead of paraphrasing indirect expressions into something more direct, you will do the opposite. Listen to the tape. On the lines below, write the words that you hear on the left, and then, by yourself or in a group, try to find ways of saying these things more indirectly. Write your indirect phrases on the right. Work quickly. After you finish, compare your results with your classmates'. The first one is done for you as an example.

1. *failing grade*   1. *less than satisfactory demonstration of learning*

2. _____   2. _____

3. _____   3. _____

4. _____   4. _____

5. _____   5. _____

6. _____   6. _____

7. _____   7. _____

8. _____   8. _____

9. _____   9. _____

10. _____   10. _____

Exercise 4—General and Specific Words

Sometimes language lacks directness or specificness because very general words are used. Exercise 10—Presentations: News at the end of chapter 4, page 42, focused on the importance of using specific language in presentations. For more practice in using specific language, listen to the general words on the tape, write them quickly below on the lines on the left, and then write more specific words, in the same category, on the right. The first two are done for you as examples.

1. *vegetable*   1. *Carrot*

2. *job*   2. *bus driver*

3. _____   3. _____

4. _____   4. _____

5. _____   5. _____

6. _____   6. _____

7. _____   7. _____

8. _____   8. _____

9. _____   9. _____

10. _____   10. _____

Continue with the exercise, but now listen to the general words and in response write only your own specific words that are in the same category. The first one is done for you as an example.

11. *dog*   16. _____

12. _____   17. _____

13. _____   18. _____

14. _____   19. _____

15. _____   20. _____

Exercise 5—Denotations and Connotations

Paraphrasing and summarizing are based on substituting words for other words. No substitution will have exactly the same meaning as the original wording. Synonyms, for example, are words with similar meanings, not words with the same meaning. The differences in meaning are often in *connotations*, which are extra meanings or associations that words may have. For example, the words *fat* and *heavy* can have the same *denotation*—they can denote, or refer to, a person who weighs more than is normal for his or her body type. However, the connotations of the words are different: *fat* sounds negative, or disapproving, while *heavy* sounds more positive, or accepting. It is important to understand possible differences in meaning when you are substituting words—when you are paraphrasing or summarizing.

In exercise 2, you generally substituted neutral words for more positive-sounding ones. In exercise 3, you did the opposite, generally substituting more positive expressions for neutral ones. In this exercise, write the two or three words that you hear for each number on the lines on the left. Then arrange the words under the columns on the right: *positive*, *neutral*, or *negative*. There is some room for disagreement about how to arrange the words, but for the most part you and your classmates should agree. The first two are done for you as examples.

	Positive	Neutral	Negative
1. job, position	position	job	
2. TV, boob tube		TV	boob tube
3.			
4.			
5.			
6.			
7.			
8.			

Continue with the exercise, but now listen to the words and write them only once, in the appropriate columns.

	Positive	Neutral	Negative
9.			
10.			
11.			
12.			
13.			
14.			
15.			

Exercise 6—Student Connotations

Choose at least three of the items below. For each, think of two or three descriptive words that are the same part of speech and that have the same denotation but that have different connotations. The connotations may be positive, neutral, or negative. Then write sentences using the descriptive words that you have thought of. Say some of your sentences in class and ask your classmates to explain the differences in connotation. Recommended parts of speech are given in parentheses. Use a dictionary only if necessary.

Example: A man *of great size* (adjectives)
He's *gigantic.* (positive)
He's *big.* (neutral)
He's *monstrous.* (negative)

Use the lines below to write your sentences.

1. A day with high temperatures (adjectives)

2. A day with low temperatures (adjectives)

3. A city with a lot of people (adjectives or nouns)

4. A conversation in which two people are disagreeing (nouns)

5. A man or woman who is the opposite of being big (adjectives or nouns)

6. A car that has been driven for many years (nouns; or adjectives and nouns together)

7. A person whose appearance (looks) is like most other people's (adjectives; or adjectives and nouns together)

8. A soccer team that plays with a lot of force and emotion (adjectives or adverbs)

9. A person without a job and a home (nouns; or adjectives and nouns together)

10. Clothes that need to be cleaned (adjectives)

11. A person who likes old ways and does not like a lot of change (adjectives or nouns)

12. A person who is very careful with his or her money (adjectives)

1. _____
_____
_____
2. _____
_____
_____
3. _____
_____
_____

Exercise 7—Discussion: The Military

In *The Case of the Roundabouts*, Brigadier General Roundabout was a career military man. Mrs. Roundabout indicated that she and her husband were both very proud of his service to their country. The questions that follow will lead you to examine your own thoughts and feelings about the military. You may want to consider these discussion questions with regard to your native country or with regard to all countries. Choose one or more questions to talk about. First, though, test your memory of expressions used for clarifying in a discussion. Write them on the lines provided. Review these expressions in order to help yourself participate well in the discussion activity.

Discussion Questions

1. Is there a need for a military? If yes, will there ever be a time when there is no need? Explain.

2. Should a country require military service—in which case some people would volunteer anyway—or rely on volunteers? What are the advantages and disadvantages of these two possibilities?

3. If military service is required, should it be for men only or for both men and women? Explain.

4. If a person refuses to serve in or support the military, does that necessarily mean that he or she is unpatriotic? Explain.

5. What should be the role of the military in a country?

6. What kinds of problems occur with the military in some countries?

7. Why is it often difficult to control the military? How can it, and should it, be controlled?

8. Must an individual obey all orders given in the military without question? Explain.

Review: Clarifying in Discussions

How many expressions used for clarifying in discussions can you remember? Only after you have checked your memory completely should you refer to the information at the end of chapter 5.

Clarifying Your Statement	Clarifying Another Person's Statement
1. _____	1. _____
2. _____	2. _____
3. _____	3. _____
4. _____	4. _____
5. _____	5. _____
6. _____	
7. _____	
8. _____	
9. _____	

Exercise 8—Presentations: Customs Related to Stages of Life

Marriage, retirement, old age, and the approach of death were important stages of life mentioned in *The Case of the Roundabouts*. Make a three-to-five-minute presentation to your classmates about a custom in your native culture that is related to some important part of life: for example, birth, reaching adulthood, choosing a career, marriage, retirement, or death. Study the information on the next page about organizing and about using specific language (with reference to the example below); it will help you to prepare for your presentation.

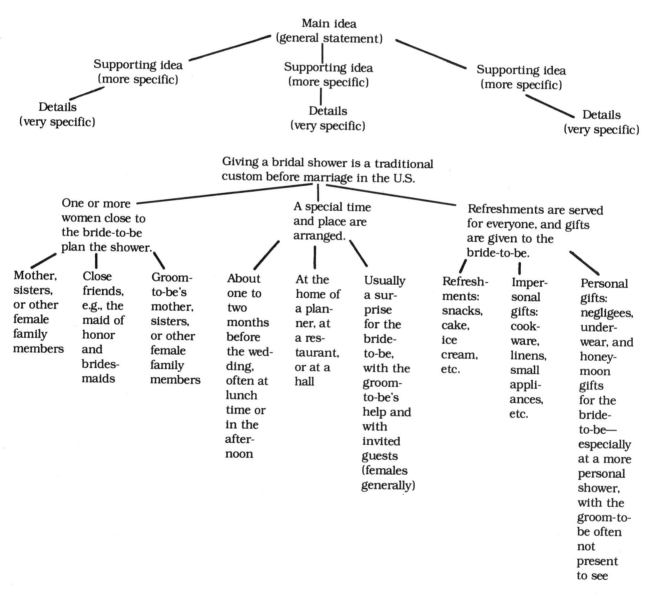

Combining Organization and Specific Language in Presentations

The presentations that you did earlier focused on (1) planning and organizing and (2) using specific language. These two areas can and should go closely together. The pyramid on the preceding page is an example of this "togetherness."

The example uses an actual presentation subject, with supporting ideas expressed in short sentences and with details expressed in phrases—in other words, an outline form. Notes like these, in a pyramid or in some other outline form, are used to help a presenter remember all the parts of his or her complete presentation.

The same general-to-specific organization of information may be achieved in a formal outline like the one below. This outline is considered less formal when the numbering and lettering are not used.

Giving a bridal shower is a traditional custom before marriage in the U.S.

I. One or more women close to the bride-to-be plan the shower.
   A. Mother, sisters, or other female family members
   B. Close friends, e.g., the maid of honor and bridesmaids
   C. Groom-to-be's mother, sisters, or other female family members

II. A special time and place are arranged.
   A. About one to two months before the wedding
   B. Often at lunchtime or in the afternoon
   C. At the home of a planner, at a restaurant, or at a hall
   D. Usually a surprise for the bride-to-be
      1. With the groom-to-be's help
      2. With invited guests (females generally)

III. Refreshments are served for everyone: snacks, cake, ice cream, etc.

IV. Gifts are given to the bride-to-be.
   A. Impersonal gifts: cookware, linens, small appliances, etc.
   B. Personal gifts: negligees, underwear, honeymoon gifts, etc.
      1. Especially at a more personal shower
      2. Groom-to-be often not present to see

7 The Case of Marooned on the Moon

Prelistening: The Situation

Everyone knew that Cosmo Pennypacker, President of Pennypacker Moon Copper, had decided in his old age to reward the people who had contributed the most to his success and happiness over the years. Everyone also knew that the people to receive the rewards would be surprised because Pennypacker did not want to tell them face to face what he was going to do for them; he did not want to cause them or himself any embarrassment.

But they had an even greater surprise first. They were shocked when Pennypacker was attacked at his space headquarters on Earth Monday evening, put into a spaceship, and rocketed to the dark side of the moon. Even worse, the villain who did this to Pennypacker used some secret computer codes for sending the spaceship, and the ship cannot be brought back unless the villain is discovered and forced to reveal the codes. Until then Pennypacker is marooned on the moon!

Sherlock Holmes, Dr. Watson, and Inspector Lestrade have been called into the case to help rescue this new version of the "old man on the moon."

Instructions

Everyone in class will have a role to play in the mystery. The three students who play Holmes, Watson, and Lestrade will ask questions and summarize the information that they receive. Because of concern for Pennypacker—and for the $25,000 reward in the case!—everyone else will also summarize the information on the chart below in order to help solve the mystery. Do not write too much. Instead, summarize only the important things. Try to use your own words as much as possible.

Your teacher will assign you a number. Quickly turn to it in the Roles and Clues section beginning on page 176 and become familiar with your role. If it seems to you that you yourself are the villain, don't show your guilt—try to escape detection!

Investigative Chart

Suspect	Time of last contact with Pennypacker	What Pennypacker is going to do for the suspect (learned from another suspect)

Questions

Answer these questions orally or in writing.

1. How many suspects are there in the case?

2. Who are the suspects?

3. When did each suspect last talk with Pennypacker?

4. What was Pennypacker going to do for each suspect?

5. For which suspect was Pennypacker apparently going to do nothing?

6. Whom do you think Pennypacker was going to fire?

7. Who do you think is the guilty person? Why?

Listening Skill: Summarizing, Continued

The listening skills of repetition and summarizing are closely related, as you may have found in working on *The Case of Marooned on the Moon*. Of course, the big difference is that with repetition you say (aloud or to yourself) the exact words that you have heard, and with summarizing you try to use fewer words, and mostly your own words, to express the main idea of what you have heard. The exercises that follow will lead you from repetition to summarizing.

Exercise 1—Moon Trip

With the other students, form a circle of seats in the classroom. Here is the class's situation: All of you have a mission. You are going to go to the moon and take something with you. The things that you will take have to be in alphabetical order, and each student has to repeat all of the things that were said before. If a student misses anything or forgets something and can't remember it in three seconds, then he or she has to stay behind. No one may write anything.

Example:

Student number 1: I'm going to go to the moon, and I'm going to take an *a*lligator.

Student number 2: I'm going to go to the moon, and I'm going to take an *a*lligator and some *b*ananas.

Student number 3: I'm going to go to the moon, and I'm going to take an *a*lligator, some *b*ananas, and a *c*ute boy.

Make sure that you use *a, an, the,* and *some* correctly, or you will have to stay behind. Go around the circle until you have gone through the alphabet once.

Exercise 2—Follow That Story

Stand up and form a long line in the classroom. (Part or all of the class may participate.) At one end of the line a student will whisper a short story or joke, two to five sentences long, in the ear of the student next to him or her. The second student will then whisper the story or joke in the ear of the next student, and so on to the end of the line. The last student in line will tell the story or joke to the whole class. How close is the final version to the first version or to other versions? If there are any changes in the story or joke, why did they occur?

Exercise 3—Summarizing Stories

Listen to the two stories on the tape. After listening to each one, pick up your pen or pencil and summarize the story briefly on the lines provided. Compare your summaries with the other students' summaries. How close are they to the original stories?

1. _____
   _____
   _____

2. _____
   _____
   _____

Exercise 4—Summarizing Student Stories

Create your own story involving outer space. Plan it carefully. You may want to write it out on the lines provided below. Tell your story to the class, but do not read what you have written. The students will summarize your story. Everyone will have a chance to tell a story and to hear it summarized. How close are the summaries to the original stories?

Your story: _____
_____
_____
_____
_____
_____
_____

Exercise 5—Summarizing from Enumeration or Linear Development

Enumeration can be helpful in summarizing, especially if there is enumeration or some clearly linear (like a straight line) development in what we hear. Listen to the proposal on the tape and complete the summary below.

There were _____ interesting ideas (or important points) in the speaker's peace proposal.

First, _____

_____

_____

Second, _____

_____

Third, _____

_____

_____

Last, _____

_____

Listen to the second short talk. Complete the summary below, or take brief notes and use the format below for giving your summary orally.

There were _____ steps to the speaker's suggestion for writing a poem.

First, _____

_____

_____

Second, _____

_____

Third, _____

_____

Finally, _____

_____

_____

Note: Your teacher may require you to do spoken or written summaries of the remaining formal presentations that students will give in class and that are based on the presentation exercises in this book. You may gain additional good practice by listening to and summarizing radio and TV news programs.

Exercise 6—Summarizing Short Student Talks

Prepare a short informal talk about one of the following: a proposal for the world, instructions about how to do something, or an experience you had over a short period of time. You may want to write your ideas briefly on the lines provided below. Use enumeration or other signal words for each part of your talk. Then give your short talk to the class. The other students may take notes, but they will give their summaries of your talk orally. Everyone will have a chance to give a talk as well as to summarize. How similar are the summaries to the talks?

Your plan for your talk: _____

_____

_____

_____

_____

_____

_____

Exercise 7—Interviews about the Unknown

In the past, explorations into the unknown have resulted in some fantastic stories, not all of them factual. These stories have generally been reported by the returning explorers, but some have come from people encountered during the explorations. Imagine that you are an explorer returning from some previously unvisited territory on earth or elsewhere, or that you are "intelligent life" from some unknown place. A classmate will interview you about your experiences, using *Wh* question words. Give him or her some fantastic answers! Your interviewer in turn will use repetition and summarizing to be sure about the fantastic information and to emphasize it. After the interview is complete, reverse roles for a second interview. Your teacher may ask you to perform one or both of these interviews in front of the class.

Use the lines below to help conduct and record the interview.

Who: _____
_____ ?
Where: _____
_____ ?
_____: _____
_____ ?
_____: _____
_____ ?
_____: _____
_____ ?
_____: _____
_____ ?
_____: _____
_____ ?

Discussion 8—Discussion: Enterprise and Responsibility

The unnamed work problems that the guilty person had in *The Case of Marooned on the Moon* involved the mining operations on the moon conducted by Penny-packer and his company. The person had questions about the right of a private company to conduct those operations and also about the potential dangers that might result in the outer and inner space environment. Read the following discussion questions; they are about space exploration and development and about enterprise in general. Choose one or more to talk about. Before you begin discussing them, however, study the information on the next page about interrupting; it can help you participate well in the discussion. Practice using these interrupting phrases and learn them.

Discussion Questions

1. Should businesses be allowed to explore and develop outer space in any way that they choose? Explain.

2. Should individual countries be allowed to explore and develop outer space in any way that they choose? Explain.

3. What are some of the potential benefits to be gained from exploring outer space?

4. What are some of the potential dangers that may be caused by space exploration?

5. If other intelligent life forms are discovered in outer space, what should be done?

6. If unintelligent life forms are discovered in outer space, what should be done?

7. How much freedom should businesses be allowed in general?

8. What should employees do if they have strong questions about or objections to the business practices of the company that employs them?

9. How much responsibility do individuals have for the things that their companies or countries do?

Interrupting in Discussions

Sometimes in a discussion, you may find that one or two people are not allowing other people—maybe you—enough chance to talk. Or you may find the need to say something that cannot wait until later. In either case, it is a good idea to *interrupt* politely, usually just as someone completes a sentence or thought and before he or she has a chance to continue talking or another person begins to speak. Below are some useful phrases to use for interrupting.

Interrupting

1. Excuse me . . .

2. Excuse me for interrupting . . .

3. I hate to interrupt, but . . .

4. I'd like to add . . .

5. If I may, I'd like to say (add, point out, etc.) . . .

6. Yes, but . . .
Okay, but . . .
Right, but . . .
(These three phrases begin more with a recognition of a speaker's words than with any kind of agreement; the "but" indicates that the interrupter is going to disagree to some extent with what has been said.)

7. Hold on.

8. Just a minute.
(These last two phrases represent a stronger interruption and indicate a stronger disagreement.)

8 The Case of the Friendly Prank

Prelistening: The Situation

Here is how Sherlock Holmes himself introduces this case: "My reputation in the world is mostly based upon my pursuit of justice. What is often overlooked is my equally strong pursuit of humor. And nothing delights me more than to see humor serve justice—an unbeatable combination as far as I am concerned. We need the lightness of humor when things become too heavy. What better way is there to lift the burdens in life that threaten to weigh us down? And one of the lightest, most uplifting little human-interest cases I ever heard of dealt with a rather burdensome young college student named Tom Comeuppance, who truly deserved the 'comeuppance' that he received . . ."

Instructions

1. Listen to the taped account of the case in order to get a general understanding of it. Then listen again, read the tapescript as you listen, and fill in the blank spaces.

2. After you finish listening and filling in the blanks, answer the questions that follow.

Tapescript

People _____ Tom Comeuppance because of all of his _____ traits— and despite his one very _____ trait. Tom is never satisfied with _____. He always finds _____ to complain about and _____ for, and he usually complains and wishes about the _____ thing for a _____ time. Most of the time, he also ends up _____ what he has been wanting, but even _____ he still finds something to _____ about soon after. This kind of _____ sometimes drives his family and friends _____.

Lately, Tom has been complaining about needing a _____ even though his _____ just recently helped him get his own _____ near the school he attends, the Merlin Institute of Technology (MIT). His _____ also got together and _____ him a ten-speed _____ for his birthday. This is what Tom has been saying:

"I'm _____ of walking and riding around so much. I need a _____. I sure wish I owned that 1965 Ford _____ that's for sale over at Bob Fisher's _____ lot."

His _____ at MIT, who are studying _____ engineering with him, are also _____—they're tired of _____ this from him so much. In fact, they can't _____ it any more. They've _____ with it long enough. In other words, they are simply _____. This is the way they let him _____ it in the cafeteria Friday afternoon.

" _____ —that's all we ever _____ from you these days. It's _____ wearing thin."

" _____ already! You sound like a broken _____!"

"Yeah, could you _____ the record, please?"

But these words didn't _____ Tom. They rolled off him like water off a _____ back. He wasn't even bothered when the _____ kind of thing happened at his _____ house, where he went for dinner on Saturday. The _____ of his family are very _____ in their jobs and interests—his father is a _____ operator, his mother is a science _____ writer, his sister is a _____ builder, and his brother is a _____—but they are all alike in _____ Tom very much. Even so, there is a _____ to how much their love can _____ from him. These were their words:

"Tom, you're starting to get on my _____ with all this car talk."

"You're really rubbing _____ the wrong way, too."

"I'll be even more _____ with you—you're going to drive me to _____!"

"Tom, you know the expression, 'Every cloud has a _____ lining'? For _____, the expression should be, 'Every silver lining has a _____.'"

On Sunday, Tom spent the whole day in the _____. When he got back to his _____ Sunday night, he found a very big and very unusual _____ waiting for him. You could have knocked him over with a _____ when he saw it. There was a _____ attached to it that read,

"_____! You've been driving _____ up a wall. Now it's _____ turn. And _____ time, for once, _____ look a _____ horse in the _____!"

Questions

Answer these questions orally or in writing.

1. What kind of person is Tom Come-uppance? What is his one bad trait?

2. What have Tom's family and friends done for him lately?

3. What has he been complaining about needing since then? Does he have a particular one in mind?

4. What are Tom and his friends studying at the Merlin Institute of Technology?

5. How have his friends responded to Tom's latest complaining?

6. What do you learn about Tom's family?

7. How have they responded to his latest complaining?

8. Does Tom usually get what he wants? Did he get what he wanted this time?

9. What was the very big and very unusual gift that Tom found in his apartment? Was it really a horse? (Consider the meaning of *mustang*.)

10. Who do you think put the gift in Tom's apartment and wrote the note? Who are the "suspects" and how do they qualify as suspects?

11. How do you think the gift giver or givers got the present into Tom's apartment?

12. Why is this prank an appropriate one to play on Tom?

Listening Skill: Guessing from Context or Requesting an Explanation

There are mysteries in everyday speech. For example, every language has interesting *idiomatic expressions*, which are special ways of communicating meaning. The meaning of an *idiomatic expression* is often different from the normal meanings of the words that make up the expression.

Look at the following two passages from *The Case of the Friendly Prank* and try to identify the idiomatic expressions.

1. "'Car, car, car'—that's all we ever hear from you these days. It's really wearing thin."

2. But these words didn't hurt Tom. They rolled off him like water off a duck's back.

When you hear an *idiom*, or just a word or short phrase that you do not understand immediately, there are two good ways to respond:

1. If there is other, helpful information, you should try to *guess the meaning* of the unknown word or words *from the context*. It is also a good idea to state your guess if you have the opportunity because someone will usually tell you if you are right, or correct you if you are wrong.

Examples:

A. So, "It's wearing thin" means something has been said or done too much. It's beginning to bother someone.
B. Yes, that's right.

A. In other words, "They rolled off him like water off a duck's back" means that he wasn't paying attention or wasn't listening.
B. Well, no, not exactly. It means he wasn't bothered or hurt at all.
A. Oh, I see. Okay. Thanks.

2. If there is not enough information from the context to help you guess the meaning, then you should *ask for an explanation*. That is a good, active listening practice.

Examples:

"Wearing thin"?

What does "wearing thin" mean?

What's "rolled off him like water off a duck's back"?

What do you mean by "rolled off him like water off a duck's back"?

"Rolled off him like water off a duck's back"? What's that? (What does that mean?) (What do you mean by that?)

Guessing from context and *requesting an explanation* are important listening skills because they are an aid to thinking in the new language, they show a conversation partner that you have been listening carefully, and they generally improve communication.

Exercise 1—Idioms from the Case

Make a list of the idioms in *The Case of the Friendly Prank*, and beneath them write your guesses as to their meanings. Compare your results in class.

1. _____
_____

2. _____
_____

3. _____
_____

4. _____
_____

5. _____
_____

6. _____
_____

7. _____
_____

8. _____
_____

9. _____
_____

10. _____
_____

11. _____
_____

12. _____
_____

13. _____
_____

14. _____
_____

15. _____
_____

16. _____
_____

Exercise 2—Guessing the Meanings of Idioms, I

Listen to the tape and write the idioms that you hear in the blank spaces below. Then guess their meanings and write them on the lines beneath.

1. _____ , I'll be ready to leave in just a minute.

_____

2. I'm afraid that Hideo _____ _____ and now everybody knows our plans.

_____

3. Ravi thought he was being funny, but the fact is his joke _____

_____

4. The basketball team is _____ _____ . They've won their last five games.

_____

5. Nui is _____ about her planned vacation in Paris.

_____

6. I was supposed to meet a new friend for dinner last night, but she _____ .

_____

7. Mr. Sato says that we have to learn to get our work done on time so he has _____ on late homework.

_____

8. Amedeo _____ with his parents because he forgot to tell them how late he would be getting home.

_____

9. Fahad should have known better what to say in that situation. He sure _____ _____ that time.

_____

10. Martin was a great soccer player for many years, but he's _____ now.

_____

11. The police strongly suspected the owner of having burned down his own store in order to collect the insurance, so they asked him to _____ them.

_____

12. Some salespeople have just the _____ —they can sell anyone anything.

_____

13. Microwave ovens cook so fast that they really _____ cooking _____ .

_____

14. Her excuse for not getting her homework done was pretty wild, but it still _____ .

_____

15. Mei-Ling _____ her homework and finished it a day early.

_____

Exercise 3—Guessing the Meanings of Idioms, II

Listen to the idioms on the tape, think about the contexts they are in, and write your best guess as to their meanings. If you cannot guess a meaning, then try to include the idiom in a request for an explanation.

1. _____
2. _____
3. _____
4. _____
5. _____
6. _____
7. _____
8. _____
9. _____
10. _____
11. _____
12. _____
13. _____
14. _____
15. _____

Exercise 4—Idioms from Students

Present to your classmates other English idioms that you have heard, and they will share some with you. Try to guess meanings, and ask for explanations when you are not able to guess correctly.

Provide a sentence context for your idioms.

1. _____
   _____
   _____
2. _____
   _____
   _____
3. _____
   _____
   _____
4. _____
   _____
   _____
5. _____
   _____
   _____

Exercise 5—Guessing the Meanings of Two-Word Verbs, I

A two-word verb is a verb and a preposition (or an adverb) that together have a special meaning. For example, in *The Case of the Friendly Prank*, there is the information that Tom "got back to his apartment Sunday night." *Get back* is a two-word verb that means "return" in this context. Some combinations include a verb plus two other words. For instance, in the story it says that Tom's friends have "put up with" his complaints about needing a car. *Put up with* means "tolerate" or "accept patiently."

Sometimes the same or nearly the same two-word verb will have different meanings in different situations. For example, *bring up* can mean (1) "to care for children until they become responsible for themselves" or (2) "to mention or introduce a subject."

Examples:

1. Just about all new parents plan to bring their children up with a lot of love.

2. Please don't bring up any more problems for discussion today!

Listen to the tape and write the two-word verbs that you hear in the blank spaces below. Then guess their meanings and write them on the lines beneath.

1. Bill likes Judy and thinks that she likes him, so he's going to _____ her _____ .

_____

2. Hong wasn't ready to answer when his teacher _____ him.

_____

3. They _____ the picnic because of bad weather.

_____

4. I _____ an interesting article in the newspaper about living under the ocean.

_____

5. A former student of mine _____ to tell me about her new job.

_____

6. Hae Sung _____ her clothes _____ at the cleaner's on her way to school.

_____

7. International and native students in the U.S. have very different backgrounds, but they usually _____ very well together.

_____

8. Holmes is _____ the facts, but he needs to investigate further.

_____

9. He always tries to _____ washing the dishes with the excuse that he has a lot of homework.

_____

10. She _____ her illness quickly and returned to work on Monday.

_____

11. He doesn't like to have blood samples taken, so he asked the nurse to _____ it _____ as quickly as possible.

_____

12. We _____ the textbook just before the final exam.

_____

13. She has trouble with math problems. Actually, her biggest problem is that she _____ on them too easily.

_____

14. She _____ the new sweater that she bought last week.

_____

15. Chen's father told him that he should _____ other people's problems.

_____

Exercise 6—Guessing the Meanings of Two-Word Verbs, II

Listen to the two-word verbs on the tape, think about the contexts they are in, and write your best guess as to their meanings. If you cannot guess a meaning, then try to include the two-word verb in a request for an explanation.

1. _____
2. _____
3. _____
4. _____
5. _____
6. _____
7. _____
8. _____
9. _____
10. _____
11. _____
12. _____
13. _____
14. _____
15. _____

Exercise 7—Two-Word Verbs from Students

In sentences that you first plan out below, present to your classmates other two-word verbs that you have heard, and they will share some with you. Try to guess meanings; ask for explanations when you are not able to guess correctly.

1. _____
   _____
2. _____
   _____
3. _____
   _____
4. _____
   _____
5. _____
   _____

Exercise 8—Discussion: Traits, Behavior, and Human Nature

In *The Case of the Friendly Prank*, we learned a lot about Tom Comeuppance's "one very bad trait" and not much about his many good traits. Read the following discussion questions; they are about traits, behavior, and human nature. Choose one or more to talk about. First, though, test your memory of phrases to use for interrupting in a discussion. Write them in the review section on the next page. Review these phrases in order to help yourself participate well in the discussion activity.

Discussion Questions

1. How do you feel about Tom Comeuppance's bad trait? Could you be friends with a person like that?

2. What good traits do you believe everyone should try to have?

3. What traits do you believe people should try to control better or eliminate?

4. What are your own good traits and bad traits?

5. What kinds of behavior are culturally determined?

6. What are some of the big differences in behavior that you see between different cultures?

7. What similarities in behavior have you seen in different cultures that may have surprised you?

8. Can you identify any universals in human behavior?

9. How would you describe human nature in general?

Review: Interrupting in Discussions

How many phrases used for interrupting in discussions can you remember? Only after you have checked your memory completely should you refer to the information at the end of chapter 7.

Interrupting

1. _____

2. _____

3. _____

4. _____

5. _____

6. _____

7. _____

8. _____

Exercise 9—Presentations: Admirable People

Make a three-to-five-minute presentation about one of the topics listed below. Remember to (1) carefully plan and organize your presentation and (2) use specific language. Note: It is common to use examples as concrete support for generalizations. Also, study the information below about visual aids; it will help you to prepare for your presentation.

Presentation Topics

1. The person or persons who have had the most positive influence on your character

2. The famous person or persons, living or dead, whose personal characteristics you admire and respect the most (you may admire one person for one thing, another person for another thing, and so on)

3. The kind of person you want to be—the traits that you want to develop and the traits that you want to diminish or eliminate

Visual Aids in Presentations

The use of *visual aids* can often help to make a presentation successful. A visual aid can be anything that gives a picture of what you say or that supports your words. Usually a visual aid helps to make your presentation more concrete for your audience.

There are many different kinds of visual aids that you may use, including the following:

1. Objects such as photographs, magazines, books, other manufactured items, or things found in the environment (to be held up in front of an audience or passed around and then returned to you)

2. Handouts for every member of the audience to keep

3. Writing on a chalkboard, on an oversized pad of paper, or on a transparency that is shown on a screen by an overhead projector

4. Slides

5. Films and video tapes

What kind of visual aid, or aids, might you use for your presentation above?

Practice using different kinds of visual aids to support your presentations. You may find some kinds more effective than others, depending on your subject and your presentation situation, or you may generally feel more comfortable with some than with others. Remember that speaking well is the most important thing and that the visual representations you use are only aids.

9 The Case of "The Material Shade"

Prelistening: The Situation

Mrs. S _____ (her last name is a secret) has come to Sherlock Holmes for help. She explains that her husband, a writer, has been made a political prisoner in their native country. She knows that before her husband was taken away from their home, he hid a valuable manuscript in which he attacks the policies of their country's government. However, even though she has been able to return to their home since then, she cannot find the manuscript. It may have been written in invisible ink or placed on microfilm, and it may be hidden in a special place in their home. Also, because the government authorities open and read all her mail before she receives it, her husband cannot tell her directly in his letters where the manuscript is.

Mrs. S _____ believes that the poem her husband just recently sent her, called "The Material Shade," contains an indirect message that tells where the manuscript is hidden. She wants Holmes to help her understand the message and find the manuscript.

Instructions

1. There are ten lines in the poem. There will be time after you hear each line for you to guess its meaning. A good way to guess is not to try to guess too much all at once. Instead, listen carefully, *repeat* each line to yourself, and try to *paraphrase* it. You may also make a question that *requests an explanation*—from yourself really—in order to focus your thinking. Doing all of these things will help your listening, thinking, and understanding. Write your responses on the numbered lines below.

2. After you have had time to respond to each line, you will hear Sherlock Holmes's response. Compare each of your responses with his to see if you have used some of the same listening skills and have come to a similar understanding of each line in the poem. After you have compared responses for all ten lines, you will have a chance to guess the manuscript's location.

Responses to the Ten Lines in the Poem

1. _____
_____
_____
_____

2. _____
_____
_____
_____

3. _____
_____
_____
_____
4. _____
_____
_____
_____
5. _____
_____
_____
_____
6. _____
_____
_____
_____
7. _____
_____
_____
_____
8. _____
_____
_____
_____
9. _____
_____
_____
_____
10. _____
_____
_____
_____

Questions

Answer these questions orally or in writing.

1. Who has come to Sherlock Holmes for help?

2. What has happened to her husband?

3. What has her husband hidden? Why?

4. In what general place is the item hidden?

5. Why can't the woman find out exactly where the item is hidden and get it?

6. What information does she have about the item's location?

7. What does she want Holmes to do?

8. Where do you think the item is hidden exactly?

9. What information helps you to make this guess?

10. Why does Holmes say that "the old light bulb just lit up for me"? What part of himself is he referring to? Is he also making a little joke? Explain.

11. Why is the hiding place that was chosen for the hidden object such a good one? What form do you think the object is in?

12. How does the poem describe the writer's life as well as the hiding place that he chose? Why do you think he wrote the poem in that way? How is the title of the poem and of the case thus appropriate?

Aha!

Listening Skill: Guessing as Interpreting

A special, deeper kind of guessing from context, called *interpreting*, is often necessary in listening. That is because language is often very figurative. That is, it is full of figures of speech, comparisons that attempt to make a message more significant, more alive, more beautiful, and ultimately more clear. Some figures of speech become part of everyday idiomatic use, so we even forget that they are figures of speech. For example, "turn off the light" does not mean that someone twists a light bulb until the electricity is disconnected. Also, is it possible to "blow out a candle" or only the flame of the candle? And does anyone really "catch a cold"? What does one use to catch it?

Some figures of speech become often-repeated, well-liked, *colorful expressions:* for example, "Your idea went over like a lead balloon." Other figures of speech that are commonly used but that do not gain the status of colorful expressions are called *tired expressions* or *cliches.* For example, "he drove like a maniac" (a crazy person) must have been a striking and even startling expression at one time, but now it has lost its freshness and interest from too much use. The difference between a colorful expression and a tired one is often very slight, a matter of opinion.

Writers and speakers who strive for thoughtful and interesting use of language try to create new figures of speech. The major, overall figure of speech in the poem "The Material Shade" is the comparison of a lamp shade (or a writer) to a spirit that is both heavily controlled and lightly valued.

Similes are figures of speech that express a similarity between two different things by using the word *like* or *as.* The "lead balloon" and "maniac" examples, above, are first of all similes—they just happen to be similes that have become commonly used.

Some similes use an "*as* + adjective + *as*" construction to name the point of similarity between the two different elements in a comparison.* Notice that the following two sentences are very close in meaning, but that the one with the "*as* + adjective + *as*" construction is specific about the point of similarity—anger.

1. He was as angry as a bear.
2. He acted like a bear.

*Note: "*As* + adverb + *as*" and "*as* + noun phrase + *as*" constructions are also used.

Exercise 1—Interpreting Common Similes

In this exercise, you will hear on the tape some of the many common similes that make comparisons between people and animals. Write the sentences that you hear on the lines below. Underline the similes and explain how they add meaning to the sentences or how they intensify the meaning. The first one is done for you as an example. (You may find that some of these similes are cliches.)

1. _She was as busy as a bee._
   Very busy— bees are very
   hard-working

2. _____

3. _____

4. _____

5. _____

6. _____

7. _____

8. _____

9. _____

10. _____

11. _____

12. _____

13. _____

14. _____

15. _____

Exercise 2—Student "As + Adjective + As" Similes

Think of your own similes that use the "*as* + adjective + *as*" construction. Below is an example, followed by some adjectives to work with. For numbers 8, 9, and 10, think of your own adjectives to work with. Share your sentences in class. Do other people fully understand the meanings of your similes?

Example:

    white: The wintry scene was as white as death.

1. red: _____

2. black: _____

3. green: _____

4. strong: _____

5. hard: _____

6. angry: _____

7. undecided: _____

8. _____ : _____

9. _____ : _____

10. _____ : _____

Exercise 3—Interpreting Original Similes, I

Listen to the sentences on the tape and write them on the lines below. Underline the similes and explain their meanings. The first one is done for you as an example.

1. *The baby's laughter sounded like bells ringing*
    Very happy—very musical

2. _____

3. _____

4. _____

5. _____

6. _____

7. _____

8. _____

9. _____

10. _____

Exercise 4—Interpreting Original Similes, II

Listen to the sentences on the tape. Pay close attention to the similes in them. Write only your explanations of their meanings on the lines below. The first one is done for you as an example.

1. *He slept well- feels great*
2. _____
3. _____
4. _____
5. _____
6. _____
7. _____
8. _____
9. _____
10. _____

Exercise 5—More Student Similes

Write five sentences of your own with similes, and write your intended meaning below each sentence. You might want to begin with common experiences and then develop striking but appropriate comparisons. For example, you might begin with things like driving in a big city, drinking a cup of coffee, watching the sun set, and so on. Tell some of your sentences in class and listen to people's efforts to explain them. Do they understand your meanings?

1. _____
   _____
2. _____
   _____
3. _____
   _____
4. _____
   _____
5. _____
   _____

Exercise 6—Interpreting Metaphors

A metaphor is a figure of speech similar to a simile. It also compares two things, but it is different in that it is often more extensive and more subtle in suggesting similar qualities. In addition, there are no words like *as* or *like* pointing out the presence of a metaphor. Compare, for example, the following four sentences:

1. He was as angry as a bear.
2. He acted like a bear.
3. He was a bear all morning.
4. He broke out of hibernation in his office, rumbling around our desks and growling orders.

We saw the first two sentences prior to exercise 1. In the first sentence, the simile specifies the similarity—anger—between two different things (a man and a bear). In the second sentence, the simile is less specific about the similarity between the two different elements, but it still focuses on behavior. It suggests acting angrily, gruffly, roughly, and so on. In the third sentence the metaphor suggests more than one similar quality between the two different elements, perhaps including angry, rough behavior but also allowing for more than that: a bearlike appearance, presence, directness, determination, aggressiveness, fierceness, and so on. The fourth sentence does not include the word "bear" at all, but there are words in it that, either alone or in this context, are associated with bears: "hibernation" (a noun), "broke out of" (a verb), and "rumbling" and "growling" (participles/adjectives). One of the two elements in the metaphor is thus less specific (because it is not stated directly), but the points of similarity lead us to understand that the comparison is with a bear.

In this exercise, you will hear on the tape some of the many common metaphors that involve comparisons between people and animals. That is, they use information about animals to express ideas about people. Write the sentences that you hear on the lines below. Underline the metaphors and explain their meanings. The first two are done for you as examples. (You may find that some of these metaphors are cliches.)

1. _She is eagle-eyed._
She sees very well —
like an eagle

2. _Why are you pecking at your_
food? Eating very little —
like a bird

3. _____
_____
_____

4. _____
_____
_____

5. _____
_____
_____

6. _____
_____
_____

7. _____
_____
_____

8. _____
_____
_____

9. _____
_____
_____

10. _____
_____
_____

Here are the animals, specific or general, that you will hear referred to indirectly in the rest of the exercise. Use this information to help you identify the metaphors and explain their meanings.

a bird   a bee (or other flying, buzzing insect)

a goat   any animal with claws for clutching, scratching, and tearing

an ostrich

11. _____
_____

12. _____
_____

13. _____
_____

14. _____
_____

15. _____
_____

You and your classmates may wish to extend the exercise and teach one another other animal metaphors that you may have learned.

Exercise 7—Interpreting Original Metaphors, I

Listen to the sentences on the tape and write them on the lines below. Underline the metaphorical parts and explain their meanings. The first one is done for you as an example.

1. *The mountains ripened in the September sunset. Turned red - like an apple*

2. _____

3. _____

4. _____

5. _____

6. _____

7. _____

8. _____

9. _____

10. _____

Exercise 8—Interpreting Original Metaphors, II

Listen to the sentences on the tape. Pay close attention to the metaphors in them. Write only your explanations of their meanings on the lines below. The first one is done for you as an example.

*1. *He got well – got rid of something unwelcome*

2. _____

3. _____

4. _____

5. _____

6. _____

7. _____

8. _____

9. _____

10. _____

*Note: A metaphor like this one, which attributes life (especially human life) to something, is often called a personification.

Exercise 9—Student Metaphors

Write five sentences of your own with metaphors, and write your intended meaning below each sentence. As you did in exercise 5, you might want to begin with common things and experiences and then develop illuminating comparisons. Tell some of your sentences in class and listen to people's efforts to explain them. Do they understand the general meanings?

1. _____
   _____

2. _____
   _____

3. _____
   _____

4. _____
   _____

5. _____
   _____

Exercise 10—Writing a Poem

Try to write a poem like "The Material Shade." For a subject, choose something very ordinary in your life. Try to look at it and understand it in different ways—use similes and metaphors to help you. Write your poem, between three and ten lines, without naming the thing. Then share your poem in class. Can others guess what you have written about?

Your poem:

_____
_____
_____
_____
_____
_____
_____
_____

Exercise 11—Discussion: Seeing in Different Ways

In *The Case of "The Material Shade,"* the writer hid his manuscript in a very clever way—he hid it in a place where everyone could see it. His action is an example of the expression, "We sometimes can't see what's in front of our faces."

Work with a classmate and discuss the picture and questions that follow. Before you begin discussing them, however, study the information on the next page about summarizing discussions; it can help you participate well in the discussion. Practice using these phrases for summarizing discussions and learn them.

Discussion Questions

1. What do the two of you see? Do you see the same thing? There are two possible perceptions. Discover what they are—solve the problem in perception by helping each other and by talking to other students if necessary.

2. Why do you think the artist drew the picture in this way? What do you think the artist is trying to tell us?

3. How does the picture relate to the expression, "We sometimes can't see what's in front of our faces"? What does that expression mean to you?

4. How are similes and metaphors useful for perception and communication? What do they help us to do?

When all of the pairs of students have finished discussing, compare your results with those of the class as a whole.

Summarizing Discussions

As well as being an important listening skill, summarizing is useful in discussions. It is like *clarifying*, but it is more useful for ensuring general understanding, and it is especially useful for concluding a discussion. The outcome of the discussion is thus not left in any question or doubt. Below are some useful phrases for summarizing a discussion.

1. So, what we are saying, then, is . . .

2. So, what we have agreed to, then, is . . .

3. Then we agree . . .

4. Basically we are in agreement . . .

5. Then we disagree . . .

6. I'm afraid we can't agree (come to an agreement) this time . . .

7. I'm afraid we have to end in disagreement . . .

8. It looks as if neither of us (none of us) is willing to change his (or her) opinion. All we can agree on is to disagree . . .

10 The Case of "Who Am I?"

Prelistening: The Situation

As a private detective, Sherlock Holmes is accustomed to helping many different kinds of individuals who come to him with many different kinds of problems. In this case, however, the individual *is* the problem. In other words, the mystery is the mysterious stranger himself!

Instructions

1. There are ten sections in the taped account of this case. There will be time after each section to think about the information in that section and to come to a conclusion about it—a possible conclusion or a more definite conclusion. Write the best idea that comes to you as quickly as you can on each numbered line below. Use *may, might,* or *could* for possible conclusions and *must* for more definite conclusions.

Examples:
>She *may* be watering the plants outside. (possible)
>He *might* be from Italy. (possible)
>They *could* have already arrived. (possible)
>She *must* be a student. (more definite)

(These examples are not related to the story.)

2. If you think you have solved the mystery before you hear all ten sections, continue to listen and write after each section in order to make sure that you are right. Also, let the other students have the pleasure of solving the mystery by themselves.

Conclusions about the Ten Sections

1. _____
2. _____
3. _____
4. _____
5. _____
6. _____
7. _____
8. _____
9. _____
10. _____

Questions

Answer these questions orally or in writing.

1. What problem did the visitor bring to Sherlock Holmes? What might have caused this problem?

2. Describe the visitor's general physical condition. What might this suggest?

3. What kinds of clothes did the visitor wear? What was most unusual about his clothes? What could this part of his appearance suggest?

4. Describe the stranger's face. What might his face tell us about his life?

5. What did the stranger remember about his work? How might this relate to the information about his appearance? What might his profession be?

6. What was unusual about the stranger's hands? What might this suggest?

7. What did he have in his pockets? What could this mean?

8. What was the stranger's other possession? What was unusual about it? What might that tell about him?

9. What names could the stranger remember? Have you heard these names before? Where? What may these names and relationships mean regarding the identity of the stranger?

10. Do we have any information about the stranger's own name? What last unusual thing did the stranger seem to remember? What might that suggest about his identity or nature?

11. What do all of these facts add up to? In other words, who must this stranger be?

Exercise 1—More Concluding

Here is another story to listen to, think over, and come to some conclusions about. Fill in the blank spaces as you listen, and then answer the questions that follow.

The Perils of Pauline

Pauline Patterson, a rancher's daughter, was _____ in _____ with Ringo Slade, the most famous _____ in the West. Last week she decided that she had to _____ to _____ as soon as possible. This was her _____:

1. Get out of her _____ bed and forget about her _____ and the sharp _____ in her side

2. Take her father's new wild _____, Firebreather, because it was the _____ on their ranch

3. Cross a _____ that was heavily populated with poisonous _____

4. Take a shortcut down a steep _____

5. Find shelter under a tall _____ when the electrical _____ that had been predicted finally _____

6. Swim across a very fast and very strong _____

7. Avoid the other _____ and the law _____ who were trying to capture or _____ Ringo

8. Watch out for Sadie Malone, Ringo's _____ girlfriend, who had already _____ two other _____ girlfriens

9. Slip her hand under Ringo's _____ while he was _____ in order to remove the _____ that he uncomfortably _____ there

Unfortunately, Pauline is now in the _____.

Questions

1. What *must* have happened to Pauline?

_____

2. What *may* have happened to her at each point in her plan?

_____

_____

_____

_____

_____

_____

_____

3. What *should* (or *shouldn't*) she have done at each point to avoid injury or illness?

_____

_____

_____

_____

_____

_____

_____

_____

Compare your answers in a small group and develop one set of answers for the group. Then compare your group's answers with those of the other groups in class.

Exercise 2—Strong Conclusions

Listen to the statements on the tape and draw a strong conclusion for each statement. Use the word *must* in your answers. The first one is done for you as an example. Compare your answers in class.

1. She *must be upset about something*
2. He _____
3. She _____
4. _____
5. _____
6. They _____
7. She _____
8. You _____
9. He _____
10. _____

Exercise 3—Possible Conclusions

Listen to the statements on the tape and draw a possible conclusion for each statement. Use *may*, *might*, or *could* in your answers. The first one is done for you as an example. Compare your answers in class.

1. *The people may be having a fight (a party)*
2. _____
3. _____
4. _____
5. _____
6. _____
7. _____
8. _____
9. _____
10. _____

Listening Skill: Inferring

Inferring, which is reaching a conclusion after considering facts or evidence, is something that we do very naturally in our first language. In a sense, inferring is a more thoughtful or definite kind of guessing. Often, this thinking process does not occur as naturally or as quickly when a second language is involved because we may be concentrating very hard on hearing direct meanings and we may miss indirect meanings or information.

People do not always say directly what they mean. They often *imply* (suggest) things and expect us to *infer* their messages (meanings). Listen to the example on the tape and fill in the blank spaces below as you listen.

Statement	Possible Response
My friend Martin needs to get a _____ , or he'll probably have to _____ school and go back _____ to his country. The problem is that his _____ aren't very good.	It sounds as if he _____ be able to _____ a scholarship and will probably have to _____ home.

There are several phrases to use to begin expressing an inference. Here is a list of some of the most common ones. You can substitute them in the Possible Response part of the conversation above.

1. It sounds as if . . .
2. So . . .
3. In other words . . .
4. I guess that means . . .
5. I suppose that means . . .
6. I'd guess from that (from what you've said) that . . .
7. Are you saying that . . . ?
8. Do you mean that . . . ?

Inferring is an advanced listening skill. You not only focus on another person's general meaning, but you also help to express it. You use your own words, make conclusions in the new language, and generally find out if your conclusions are correct. In conversation, inferring shows the other person that you have been listening carefully and thinking with him or her—communication is on a high level.

Exercise 4—Inferring Messages, I

Listen to the statements on the tape, fill in the blank spaces below as you listen, and try to infer the speakers' messages. Use the phrases for inferring listed above. The first item is done for you as an example.

1. My boss told me that if I wanted to __work__ for our company in Japan next _September_, then I should have _talked_ to him about the possibility back in _March_ .
Message: _I guess that means you won't be able to go there to work._

2. Some _____ are worth paying _____ dollars to see. Others are worth about _____ that much. Tonight's _____ should have gone for about _____ cents, or less.
Message: _____
_____

3. When it's raining cats and dogs, it's raining really _____, right? Yesterday, Diane's _____ said that it was raining _____ .
Message: _____
_____

4. Husbands sometimes refer to their _____ as the "better half." Together, of course, they make a _____, but the husbands like to make this little compliment. Thomas is _____—he refers to his wife as the better _____ .
Message: _____
_____

5. They say that what goes _____ must come _____. In that case, Pandit had better get a safety net ready for his high _____ .
Message: _____

6. My husband went _____ with his friends this morning. He promised me a fresh-fish _____ for tonight. A promise is a _____. Do you know any good seafood _____ in town?
Message: _____
_____

7. Ann kept _____ about needing to get that _____ of hers into a garage for some _____. Well, a friend of mine called a few minutes ago to tell me that he saw her _____ this morning on the other side of the _____ .
Message: _____
_____

8. My cat has a bad _____. He either fell out of a _____, or he got _____ there. Of course he has been _____ a lot with the other _____ in the neighborhood.
Message: _____
_____

9. Ahmed told me that either he gets a _____ on the final exam or he _____ the course. But he also told me that he hasn't _____ very much.
Message: _____
_____

10. Some say that it's _____ to have too many hopes and _____. Others say that the alternative is a very dull way of _____. I lean toward _____ myself.
Message: _____
_____

Exercise 5—Inferring Messages, II

Listen to the statements on the tape and write only what you infer from them—what you think the real messages are. Use the phrases for inferring that you have studied. The first item is done for you as an example.

1. *So the Rijos have moved away*

2. _____

3. _____

4. _____

5. _____

6. _____

7. _____

8. _____

9. _____

10. _____

Exercise 6—Inferring Messages from Student Statements

On the lines below, plan some statements from which your classmates will have to infer your meaning. Make sure that you provide enough information for them to be able to infer. People's efforts to infer are not always successful; if your classmates do not understand your meaning, simply help them as you would in a regular conversation.

1. _____

2. _____

3. _____

Exercise 7—Extended Inferring

1. You are going to hear one-half of a telephone conversation on the tape. Listen carefully and try to infer what the conversation is about. Write your answer on the lines below.

_____

_____

2. Now you will hear one-half of another telephone conversation. Again, listen carefully and try to describe what the conversation is about.

_____

_____

As you listen to both conversations again, orally infer the content of *each part* of the conversation that you do not hear. You will be able to do this from the parts (the responses) that you do hear. (Note: If you wish to spend more time and effort, you can choose to complete the two conversations in writing.)

Exercise 8—Discussion: Communication

As this chapter has demonstrated, indirect or implied messages and inferring are an important part of communication. Actually, understanding another person's words and thoughts, making ourselves clear, and achieving real communication are not always easy to do! Read the discussion questions about communication and choose one or more to talk about. First, though, test your memory of phrases for summarizing a discussion. Write them in the review section on the next page. Review these phrases in order to help yourself participate well in the discussion activity.

Discussion Questions

1. Why aren't all of our messages clear and complete, and all of our efforts at communication easily and completely successful?

2. What would life be like if everything we said were clear and obvious?

3. What things are especially difficult to be clear and direct about?

4. In what areas is clear communication absolutely necessary?

5. If communication in a shared native language is often difficult, what factors make communication between people from different countries, with different languages, even more difficult?

6. How do governments deal with problems in communication in their contacts with one another?

Review: Summarizing Discussions

How many phrases for summarizing discussions can you remember? Only after you have checked your memory completely should you refer to the information at the end of chapter 9.

1. _____
2. _____
3. _____
4. _____
5. _____
6. _____
7. _____
8. _____
   _____

Exercise 9—Presentations: "Bad Guys"

The subject of "bad guys," real-life or fictional, is one that commands a lot of our attention. In real life, societies must decide how to deal with lawbreakers. At the same time, in both real life and in fiction, we are often fascinated by the personalities and the exploits of different kinds of "bad guys." For example, a song entitled "Ladies Love Outlaws" could well accompany the story of Pauline Patterson's love for Ringo Slade in the first exercise in this chapter.

Make a five-to-seven-minute presentation about one of the following topics dealing with "bad guys" or "bad behavior." Remember to (1) carefully plan and organize your presentation, (2) use specific language, and (3) offer visual aids if appropriate and helpful. Also, study the information below about body language; it will help you to prepare for your presentation.

Presentation Topics

1. Real-life and fictional "bad guys" that have fascinated people, including your own favorite or favorites if you have any

2. The reasons that certain "bad guys" fascinate or interest people, often more than "good guys" do (1 and 2 may be done separately or together)

3. The reasons for people's interest in crime and horror stories in newspapers, magazines, books, and movies

4. The proper focus of justice: (a) punishment of a criminal for that person's crime, (b) rehabilitation so that the criminal can return to society as a responsible and contributing member, or (c) restitution, in which the criminal is required to make good the loss or damage experienced by his or her victims (individuals, institutions, or society)

5. Whether or not capital punishment—the death penalty—should be part of society

6. An analysis of the responsibility for crimes—how much lies with an individual and how much lies outside an individual's control (for example, you may wish to consider the society around the person as being responsible to some degree)

Body Language in Presentations

Body language can be an important part of a presentation. In other words, we communicate with our bodies as well as with words. Here is a list of do's and don'ts to follow in English-speaking situations, especially in a classroom.

1. Stand with good, natural, and comfortable posture. It is generally most effective to stand in front of an audience unless there is a specific reason for sitting or the situation is informal.

2. Do not stay for too long behind a barrier like a desk, unless it is a very formal presentation. It is friendlier to the audience to come in front of the desk, even if only briefly.

3. Move around occasionally to help keep the audience's interest, especially during a long presentation. For example, if you use the chalkboard in the front of a classroom, you may move between it and the teacher's desk, which is often in front also.

4. Do not fold your arms across your chest. That looks insecure or unfriendly. Let your arms hang naturally.

5. Use gestures to support your presentation. For example, you may want to use one arm and hand to point to something (possibly on the chalkboard) for emphasis. Your teacher may demonstrate common arm and hand movements used by native English speakers, or you may learn them from careful observation.

6. Look at your audience. In English-speaking situations, it is friendlier and more communicative to make some eye contact with people.

7. Be aware of your facial expressions in general. Showing your own interest in your subject, your self-confidence, and the kinds of expressions that support your speaking will make the presentation more interesting for your audience and more effective overall.

11 The Case of the President's Hot Seat

Prelistening: The Situation

In his line of work, Sherlock Holmes deals with hard facts—he begins with some, seeks to add others, and then tries to infer any that are missing. That is the way he works at getting the total picture of a case and solving it. When he is confronted with the so-called supernatural, he immediately tries to find the concrete reality in it. The present case confronts him with just that kind of problem. He must find out (1) whether or not the president of a large university is the victim of supernatural forces, (2) who is behind the attacks that make him a victim, and (3) why the attacks are being made.

Instructions

1. Listen to the taped account of the case in order to get a general understanding of it. Then listen again, read the tapescript below as you listen, and fill in the blank spaces. This will help you to focus on important details in the situation. At this point, can you answer the three questions above that confront Sherlock Holmes? (If you think you have the solution to the case at any time before other students do, do not reveal it—instead, let them have the pleasure of solving the mystery also.)

2. After you have had some time to think alone, your teacher will ask you to discuss the information in the case with a small group of your classmates. Can your group arrive at a solution? (Remember to let students outside your group have the pleasure of solving the mystery on their own.)

3. After you have had some time for group discussion, your teacher will assign you and each of the other students in class an individual number for locating a clue to the mystery in the Roles and Clues section beginning on page 176. Your teacher may even assign you more than one number, depending on the size of the class. In your group, discuss the new information that all of you have received. Can your group solve the mystery now?

4. If you still need more information, then "negotiate" with one or more of the other groups for the information they have. Maybe those students will tell you a new clue if you tell them one—that is one possibility. Get as much information as you need from the other groups in order to solve the case.

Tapescript

A. Mr. Holmes, my name is William Hardacre. I'm the new _____ of Meriweather University, and I have a terrible _____ that I hope you can _____ me with.

B. Very well, I'll try.

A. Well, I realize that I've caused some _____ on campus, but I didn't think I had created any grounds for _____ or violence. This is what has happened. During the past two weeks, three _____ have appeared out of nowhere on my office _____. I have sat down and _____ them, and each time I have found a _____ telling me to _____ my job. Much worse, I have also found each time a _____ of a doll looking like me with first one, then two, and most recently three _____ stuck in its buttocks. At the very same moment, I have experienced a terrible sharp _____ in the same part of _____ body. A _____ pain each time.

B. Yes, I see, a case of _____ a pain in the, as you say, "_____." Do you have any idea _____ you are receiving these letters?

A. No, not exactly. Well, I know I'm not a _____ president. Among other things, I've had to make some tough _____ because of all the financial _____ the university is in. I've even been accused of practicing "_____ economics."

B. You mean following economic _____ that seem to be based more on wishes for some kind of _____ cure than on realistic thinking.

A. Yes, of course, although _____ obviously don't _____ it that way myself. Now, my _____ proposal has created the _____ uproar of all. I've proposed that the university _____ students' tuition by _____ and also _____ the salaries of teachers and staff by the _____ amount.

B. I can see where you're _____ very _____. Mr. Hardacre ...

A. *President* ...

B. Excuse me, _____ Hardacre, could you tell me _____ was in your office on the _____ you received your most recent _____ letter?

A. I think there were only _____ people who came in before I found the letter around _____. Jim Rainberry, the head of _____ on campus, was in at _____ to review maintenance _____ and what they'd _____. I also got him to do some work on the _____ _____ behind my desk that I've been having _____ with.

B. Please go on. Who else?

A. Well, at _____ I had a _____ with Lawrence Grapesun. He's a professor of electrical _____ and also the chairman of the teacher and staff _____ on campus. He wanted to express the union's _____ regarding my proposed cut in salaries.

B. After that?

A. Well, Melanie Snowden, the cafeteria _____, brought my lunch over at _____, as she usually does, so that I can keep _____ at my desk. Then Windy Peartree, my _____, brought me a cup of coffee from the outer office around _____. And that's all.

B. Very good. I'm beginning to get the _____.

A. Mr. Holmes, I am not a _____ man by nature, and I don't like the idea of being _____ to quit, but it seems to me that _____ forces are at work—forces that are out to _____ me. Here, see for _____ what was written across yesterday's photograph—" _____ is for the _____ you do!"

B. Yes, I see. I will need to make some more _____, but don't worry. I think we can get you _____ of—how shall I put it?—the " _____ seat" you've been in.

Questions

Answer these questions orally or in writing.

1. Who is William Hardacre?

2. When did he start receiving hate mail?

3. What have been the contents of the hate mail?

4. What has Hardacre physically experienced that shows the hate mail is serious?

5. Why are these things happening to Hardacre?

6. What special connection do you think exists between Hardacre's brand of economics and the threatening and painful experiences he has had?

7. Which people were in Hardacre's office on the day that he was last threatened?

8. What did these people do in his office?

9. Explain the behind-the-scenes actions in the case: How did the perpetrators come together, plan their activities, and carry them out?

10. What were all the possible motives in the case?

11. How was pain administered to Hardacre?

12. Do you think Sherlock Holmes took this case completely seriously? Why or why not?

Listening Skill: Inferring by Small Steps or by Big Jumps

The Case of the President's Hot Seat is related to other cases in this book. In *The Case of the Missing Bracelet*, the emphasis was on listening for important details and ideas. The step-by-step process of focusing on details and thinking about them was emphasized, and that "thinking in small steps" was an early introduction to one kind of inferring.

There were also steps or sections in *The Case of "Who Am I?"*, but they were much bigger steps—you were even encouraged to "jump to conclusions" in a reasonable way. That is another way that inferring often occurs—by big jumps.

With the present case, you may have proceeded by small steps, by big jumps, or by both. In the small-step process, you consciously *analyze*, or think about, the parts of something and then you *synthesize*, or put parts together, in order to arrive at a conclusion. In the big-jump process, something very similar happens, but it may seem to happen more automatically, without your consciously thinking about it, and perhaps without your considering as many parts. Think back to your work on the case. How did you proceed?

Practicing both the step-by-step and the big-jump processes can be fun and can help you to improve your ability to appreciate English and to operate in it. Several word-game exercises follow in which you may experience further these different kinds of thinking. For which exercises is your thinking more conscious and for which is it more automatic?

Exercise 1—Solving Riddles

A fruit clue may have helped in solving *The Case of the President's Hot Seat.* Here are some other fruit clues and also vegetable clues—actually they are riddles, which play with words and ideas—that should be "food for thought." Listen to the sentences on the tape and try to guess the fruit or vegetable that is described. The list that follows may help you.

beets	chili	squash
cabbage	eggplant	tangelo
cantaloupe	lettuce	watermelon
carrot	orange	
cauliflower	pear	
celery	peas	

1. _____   4. _____
2. _____   5. _____
3. _____   6. _____

Exercise 2—Creating Riddles

With another student or with a small group of students, try to write some riddles of your own for the fruits and vegetables in the following list. Work with the parts of the words and with other words that sound similar but have different meanings. Use your English dictionary if it will help you.

beets	honeydew	strawberries
blueberries	olive	tangelo
cabbage	pear	watermelon
cantaloupe	prune	
carrot	raisin	
eggplant	squash	

1. _____
   _____?
2. _____
   _____?
3. _____
   _____?

Tell your riddles to your classmates. Can they guess the answers?

Exercise 3—Mystery Word, I

Select five words from the list below. Then
stand back to back with a classmate, and
give him or her clues that are one word or
several words in length until he or she
guesses each mystery word. The team that
gets five correct answers the fastest, within
a one-minute time limit, is the winner.

Change roles with your partner and play
again. Your class may wish to use each
team's combined times to determine the
winner.

door	hamburger	car	apartment	notebook
dog	sister	class	red	soap
stereo	Monday	milk	elephant	sheets
teacher	grass	walk	coffee	table
restaurant	shoes	chalkboard	movie	TV
letter	mother	cat	sleep	chicken
socks	pizza	doctor	banana	wife
carpet	Arabic	tree	paper	mirror
closet	moon	blouse	pencil	ocean
window	Japan	rain	happy	cook
breakfast	shower	train	towel	supermarket
baby	eyeglasses	sofa	pillow	grandfather
good-bye	drive	vacation	afternoon	money
mountain	read	hair	cloudy	rice
leg	ring	egg	soccer	alarm clock
curtains	basketball	homework	rug	cry
grammar	nose	bird	quiet	orange juice
month	picture	river	lie	school
thanks	box	hat	swim	loud
watch	ride	sad	dentist	sing
handsome	peace	holiday	July	angry
love	radio	dance	visit	police officer
grade	steak	learn	computer	sentence
criminal	mystery	street	hour	mathematics
ice cream	air	gold	hill	fly

Exercise 4—Mystery Word, II

There is another way to play Mystery Word. First, divide the class into pairs. Then, the teacher will give one student in each pair the same word, and each of those students will give a one-word clue to his or her partner. The partner will then try to guess the mystery word.

Each contestant must give a clue or a response within five seconds. The team that tries first to identify the mystery word and succeeds will earn ten points. If that team fails, the team that tries second and succeeds will earn nine points, and so on down to one point. If there are fewer than ten teams, a team may have a second try at giving a clue and guessing the word. After a team guesses a word, the teacher will select a new word and the contestants will follow the same procedure, with a different team trying first. Partners alternate in giving and receiving clues for each new word. The first team to earn twenty-one points is the winner.

Exercise 5—Playing with Anagrams

An anagram is a word that is made from another word by rearranging its letters. For example, the word *smile* can be made from the letters in the word *miles*. Listen to the words on the tape. On the lines below, write each word that you hear on the left, and then make an anagram of the word and write it on the right. For some words, there may be more than one possible anagram. Complete this exercise by yourself, with a partner, or in a small group. The first one is done for you as an example.

1. *name*   1. *mean (mane)*
2. _____   2. _____
3. _____   3. _____
4. _____   4. _____
5. _____   5. _____
6. _____   6. _____
7. _____   7. _____
8. _____   8. _____

Continue with the exercise, but now do not write the words that you hear. Write only anagrams of those words.

9. _____
10. _____
11. _____
12. _____
13. _____
14. _____
15. _____

Exercise 6—Word Multiplication

Another game, similar to making anagrams, is to make as many words as possible with the letters in one word. Here is an example with the word *team*.

team: am eat ma tam
  at mat tame
  ate mate tea
  me
  meat
  met

Make as many words as you can from the letters of each of the words that you hear on the tape. Write the words on the lines on the left as you hear them, and then write the words that you think of in the spaces on the right. You will have two minutes to work on each word that you hear.

Note: You may want to work on some of the dictated words by yourself and on other words with a partner or with a small group.

1. _____:

2. _____:

3. _____:

4. _____:

5. _____:

Exercise 7—Inferring Categories, I

Listen to the groups of words on the tape. After listening to each group, write the name of the category to which the words belong. For example, if you hear *cow*, *pig*, *chicken*, *sheep*, *goat*, you might infer the category *animals* or, ever better, *farm animals*.

1. _____   7. _____

2. _____   8. _____

3. _____   9. _____

4. _____   10. _____

5. _____   11. _____

6. _____   12. _____

Exercise 8—Inferring Categories, II

Listen to the groups of words on the tape. Identify (1) the category for each group and (2) the one word that does not belong to the category.

1. _____   _____

2. _____   _____

3. _____   _____

4. _____   _____

5. _____   _____

6. _____   _____

7. _____   _____

8. _____   _____

9. _____   _____

10. _____   _____

11. _____   _____

12. _____   _____

Exercise 9—Discussion: Superstitiousness

Superstitiousness was at the center of *The Case of the President's Hot Seat* despite President Hardacre's claim that he was not superstitious. Superstitiousness may also be an important part of life in general. Read the following discussion questions and choose one or more to talk about. Before you begin discussing them, however, study the information below about approaches to "discussion as argument;" it can help you participate well in the discussion. Practice following the approaches and learn them.

Discussion Questions

1. What superstitions do you have or have you had?

2. What superstitions are common in your native country or culture? How similar are they to superstitions in other countries and cultures?

3. Some people argue that everyone is superstitious to some degree. Do you agree or disagree? Explain.

4. Is there anything "superstitious" about some of our daily habits—for example, putting our clothes on and taking them off in the same particular order every day? Why do we have those habits? How do you define superstitiousness?

5. Why are people superstitious?

6. What do superstitions offer people in life? What is the value of superstitions, if any?

7. Is there any harm in being superstitious? At what point is it harmful?

Discussion as Argument: Approaches

Discussions often take the form of an *argument.* An argument in this sense does not mean a verbal fight or an emotional disagreement. Instead, it refers to a discussion in which the focus is on trying to determine what should be believed (what is true) or what should be done (what action is best). In an argument, there are clearly different positions on a subject, and the arguer's effort is to try to convince others to agree with his or her position.

If people merely assert their own positions on a subject, no one will change and nothing will result. That happens sometimes, understandably. However, the main objective in an argument should be to use *reason* to arrive at a mutually agreed upon solution to a problem.

The question that still remains is how does one argue successfully—how does one use reason and convince others to change their positions and agree with one's own position. There are three common approaches which are described below. The examples are taken from an argument about whether or not there should be grades in school.

1. Try to find a common ground, especially a common underlying ground. Try to show that because there is agreement on a deeper or closely related matter, there should be agreement on the matter at hand as well.

Example: "I favor grades. You don't. You believe that learning, not grades, is what's important. And that's where I think you're getting at a deeper level on which we both agree—learning *is* the most important thing. The function of grades is simply to show *how much learning has taken place.* Then we can plan for and accomplish *more learning.* So, you see, because we both stress the importance of learning, and because grades support the learning process, I think you should recognize the value of having grades."

2. Try to anticipate opposing points. Address them in advance, if possible, so that opposition will be reduced. Or at least be prepared to respond to opposing points rather than saying little or nothing when those points are made.

Example: "I know you're going to say that grades are overemphasized. The fact is that some people do treat grades more as an end than as a means to an end. That's too bad. But the problem is *with those people, not with grades.* They need to learn or understand better the proper value of grades."

3. Assume a positive bearing—that is, a sense of having a position but also of being willing to discuss the issue in order to arrive at a reasonable solution. Do not be overbearing, giving the impression that you are completely right and everyone else is completely wrong. Since your attitude is more open or more questioning in this approach, use the kinds of questions that, when answered, will lead others in your direction or to your position. This is sometimes referred to as the Socratic method, named after the ancient Greek philosopher Socrates.

Example: "I enjoy discussing grades with you. And, you know, as we've gotten into the subject, a question has come to mind that I think is important for both of us to think about. It's this: Where did the idea of grades come from in the first place? I mean, what purposes have they been serving all these years?"

12 The Case of the Green Eyes, or "Isle Be Seeing You"

Prelistening: The Situation

In this case, Sherlock Holmes has the opportunity to solve a crime of the heart at the same time that he solves a crime of theft. The "bad guy" in the case has acted as if he cared about a young woman only so that he could steal from her. If Holmes can return the young woman's stolen earrings, he will also go a long way toward returning her stolen heart.

Instructions

1. Listen to the taped account of the case in order to get a general understanding of it. Then listen again, read the notes about the case and the letter from it as you listen, and fill in the blank spaces. You may use exact words from the tape for some blanks in the notes, but for others you should summarize or paraphrase. You may also want to use abbreviations so that you can more easily keep up with the tape. For the letter at the end of the notes, you will need to fill in the blanks with actual words from the tape because the letter represents information that should not be changed in any way. (If you think you have the solution to the case at any time before other students do, do not reveal it—instead, let them have the pleasure of solving the mystery also.)

2. After you have had some time to think alone, your teacher will ask you to discuss the information in the case with a small group of your classmates. Can your group arrive at a solution? (Remember to let students outside your group have the pleasure of solving the mystery on their own.)

3. After you have had some time for group discussion, your teacher will assign you and each of the other students in class an individual number for locating a clue to the mystery in the Roles and Clues section beginning on page 176. Your teacher may even assign you more than one number, depending on the size of the class. In your group, discuss the new information that all of you have received. Can your group solve the mystery now?

4. If you still need more information, then "negotiate" with one or more of the other groups for the information they have. Maybe those students will tell you a new clue if you tell them one—that is one possibility. Get as much information as you need from the other groups in order to solve the case.

The following abbreviations appear in the case notes. Remember to consider using your own abbreviations.

w/ = with   D = Drummond
exp = experience   H = Holmes
apt = apartment

Case Notes

Harriet Beechcroft—rich woman, w/
_____ exp
   Boyfriend Drummond

   Emerald Isle _____ → _____!
      _____ emeralds _____ Ireland
      Value—$ _____
Police:
   Say _____ really Willie Filcher
   History of _____
   Wanted to _____ D—but _____
   Found D's apt _____
   Everything _____
   D's partners wanted _____
Holmes & Beechcroft visit _____
   Find two _____
     1. Miss Lonelyhearts _____ in
        newspaper _____
          Name "Emma" _____ on _____
     2. Photo of _____ Raleigh in _____
        D's _____
   H's "guess":
   D hid _____
   D will communicate through _____
   _____

Miss L. letter

Dear Miss Lonelyhearts:

I'm looking for a woman who will help me _____ my life. She should be distantly _____, coolly _____, mysteriously _____-_____—all like a cat. I would also like someone whose hair is _____ blonde, a hot and cool color at the same time. That is my dream woman in terms of _____ . In terms of _____ , she should be the kind of person who _____ get into any _____ or get _____ into any trouble. I _____ want to end up in a _____ again, where too many _____ women have led me _____ .

I'm so desperate to _____ this dream woman that I'll even list my _____ number in the paper, just so that she can call me: _____ .

As for me, I'm handsome, intelligent, and wealthy—a _____ of a guy. Please call.

               Isle be _____ you,
               GD

Questions

Answer these questions orally or in writing.

1. What problem has Harriet Beechcroft brought to Sherlock Holmes?

2. What is Georgie Drummond's real identity?

3. Why can't Drummond return to his apartment?

4. What clue does Holmes find in the newspaper in Drummond's apartment?

5. What connection does the newspaper clue have to a photograph in Drummond's apartment?

6. The letter to Miss Lonelyhearts in the next day's newspaper is signed "GD." Who is GD?

7. It is unusual to see a telephone number listed in a letter of that kind. How is the telephone number significant?

8. At the end of his letter, GD describes himself as a "jewel of a guy," and he uses the closing, "Isle be seeing you." Is there any significance in his use of these words? Explain.

9. What special uses does Holmes make of the color green at the end of the story? What other associations does the color green have in the story? Why is the title appropriate?

10. Explain the behind-the-scenes action in the case: What did Drummond do after he stole the earrings from Ms. Beechcroft?

11. How did you proceed in solving the case—by small steps, big jumps, or both?

Listening Skill: Inferring Word Play

A pun is a kind of joke that involves playing with words. That is, a pun takes words that sound alike but that have different meanings and uses them in such a way that the meanings cross or exist at the same time. For example, a student who gets back a composition with a lot of red corrections from his teacher might say, "I know Mr. Smith *read* my paper, but did he have to make it this colorful?" The play in that sentence is between "read" and "red," as if Mr. Smith both read and "red" (reddened or colored with red) the student's paper. In other words, the expected meaning of "read" in the sentence is "to get the meaning of written information," and the extra or unexpected meaning is "to redden."

Sometimes different meanings of the same word cross or exist together. (It may be that two different words, but with the same spelling, are involved.) For example: "It makes sense for librarians to *book* their own travel reservations." The expected meaning of "book" in the sentence is "to arrange"; the extra meaning is "a type of reading material (found in libraries)."

There is a kind of implying and inferring involved with word play. The speaker implies or suggests more than one meaning, and those meanings often make a comment about life or language. The comment may have some seriousness in it, as in the *read/red* example above, or it may be mostly silly. The listener is expected to infer or understand all of this.

The exercises that follow will lead from simple to sophisticated word play of different kinds. Once again, practice with inferring can be fun and can help you to improve your ability to appreciate English and to operate in it.

Exercise 1—Homonyms

Homonyms, words that sound the same but that have different meanings and usually different spellings, are the basis for a lot of word play. For the list of words that you hear on the tape, try to recognize the homonyms—that is, the two differently spelled words that have the same pronunciation. There may even be more than two in some cases. Write your homonyms on the lines below. The first one is done for you as an example.

1. *Sale - sail*
2. _____
3. _____
4. _____
5. _____
6. _____
7. _____
8. _____
9. _____
10. _____
11. _____
12. _____
13. _____
14. _____
15. _____

Exercise 2—Student Homonyms

The class will be divided into small groups, and each group will make a list of as many other homonyms (beyond those in exercise 1) as it can think of. Which group makes the longest list?

Your group's list:

Exercise 3—Word Play in Sentences, I

As you listen to the sentences on the tape, fill in the blank spaces below. In each sentence, circle the main word whose sound and meaning you believe is being played with, and give a brief explanation on the line beneath. Remember the two methods of word play that were described above. The first two numbers are done for you as examples. Note: If you find any of the puns to be bad jokes, which is often the case, then the natural thing to do is groan!

1. There was so much _Snow_ on our TV screen that the repairperson had to use a _Shovel_ to fix it.
Explanation: _We expect "snow" meaning "spots", but "snow" that falls from the sky is also suggested._

2. Poor Miss _Lonelyhearts_—the only _male_ companionship she gets is from the _letter carrier_.
Explanation: _We expect "male", but mail (letters) is also suggested_

3. A woman in line at the _____ asked me if she could go _____ me, so I had to tell her I wasn't for _____.
Explanation: _____
_____
_____

4. A _____ pencil will show you the _____ way.
Explanation: _____
_____
_____

5. When he asked, "What's _____?" I responded, "_____!"
Explanation: _____
_____
_____

6. Anna thought she had caught a _____, but then it _____.
Explanation: _____
_____
_____

7. Is it true that all _____ players reach their _____ in life?
Explanation: _____
_____
_____

8. A shoplifter who has _____ thoughts about his crime will most likely _____ a business.
Explanation: _____
_____
_____

9. Instead of a new _____ reigning, the people had hoped for a long _____ spell.
Explanation: _____
_____
_____

10. Dr. Frankenstein is ambitious and would like to get _____, but his assistant likes the _____ he already has.
Explanation: _____
_____
_____

Exercise 4—Word Play in Sentences, II

Listen to the sentences on the tape and write only your brief explanations of the word plays that you hear. The first two are done for you as examples. Note: Do not groan too loudly!

1. _We expect "son," but "sun" (a star!) is also suggested._

2. _We expect "run" meaning "a hole," but "run" meaning "a race" is also suggested._

3. _____
   _____

4. _____
   _____

5. _____
   _____

6. _____
   _____

7. _____
   _____

8. _____
   _____

9. _____
   _____

10. _____
    _____

Exercise 5—Student Word Plays

Think of three sentences of your own with word plays. You can refer to the homonyms in exercises 1 and 2 to help you. You can also use individual words that have different meanings (like "book," "snow," and "run" in the examples above). Plan your sentences on the lines below, and then share them in class. Do people understand them? Do they laugh or groan?

1. _____
   _____

2. _____
   _____

3. _____
   _____

Exercise 6—Inferring Implied Messages in Literature

Poetry and stories are kinds of extended word plays that generally contain a hidden or implied message. We have to think carefully about that message in order to discover or understand it. In other words, literature suggests meanings about life. Actually, life itself often provides less obvious or less direct meanings than literature, and literature exists to help us to understand life better and to appreciate it more. With both life and literature, we look and listen carefully, we learn to understand and to appreciate, and we take pleasure in our experience.

Listen to the two poems and the story on the tape. For the poems, fill in the blank spaces below. For the story, just listen. Try to discover or understand their messages. If you have any trouble understanding, answering the questions after each work will be helpful. Discuss your ideas with your classmates.

Living Tenderly

My body a rounded _____
with a pattern of smooth seams.
My head a short _____,
retractive, projective.
My legs _____ of their sleeves
or shrink within,
and so does my _____.
My eyelids are quick clamps.
My back is my _____.
I am always at _____.
I travel where my _____ walks.
It is a smooth stone.
It floats within the _____,
or rests in the _____.
My flesh lives tenderly
inside its _____.

Questions

1. What is the shape of the speaker's body?

_____

2. What does its head look like?

_____

3. In what unusual way do its legs move?

_____

4. What is unusual about its house (home)?

_____

5. What kinds of places can it be in?

_____

6. True or false: like our bodies, its bone is inside its flesh?

_____

7. What is described in the poem—who is the speaker?

_____

Metaphors

I'm a _____ in nine syllables,
An _____, a ponderous _____,
A melon strolling on two tendrils.
O red _____, ivory, fine timbers!
This _____ big with its yeasty rising.
Money's new-minted in this fat _____.
I'm a means, a stage, a _____ in calf.
I've eaten a bag of green _____,
Boarded the _____ there's no
    getting off.

Questions

1. How many syllables are in each line?

2. How many lines are there in the poem?

3. How many metaphors are there in the poem? ("Melon" and "red fruit" are one, as are the three things in line 7.)

4. Why is the number in answer to 1, 2, and 3 significant?

5. What things does this speaker compare herself to?

6. Does the seventh metaphor, in line 7, come closest to describing the speaker's situation? Explain.

7. Does the speaker have different feelings about her situation? Explain.

8. Can you understand the speaker's feelings? Discuss.

After listening to the story entitled "A Parable," on the tape, answer the questions below. You may wish to read the questions first in order to help you focus your attention.

1. How many dangers is the man facing? Explain.

2. What is going to happen to the man?

3. Do you think the color of the mice has any special meaning? Explain.

4. What does the man do in his terrible situation?

5. How can the man enjoy what he does in this situation?

6. Do you think the color of the strawberry has any special meaning? Explain.

7. What is the story trying to tell us—what is its message?

8. How would you describe the feeling (the tone) of the story?

Exercise 7—Discussion: Love

Love is something that the world cannot stop thinking about, writing about, talking about, singing about, looking for, fighting over, and so on. Read the following discussion questions about love and choose one or more to talk about. First, though, test your memory of useful approaches to "discussion as argument"; describe them in the review section of the next page. Review these approaches in order to help yourself participate well in the discussion activity.

Discussion Questions

1. What is love? How many different kinds of love are there?

2. Is there a difference between romantic love and committed love? Explain.

3. Which is more important—loving or being loved? Explain.

4. Should other people, for example parents, help young men and women meet and decide whether or not to marry? Explain.

5. What is your opinion of modern methods used to meet a potential boyfriend or girlfriend (or marriage partner)—for example, personal advertisements, dating services (including the use of computers), singles bars, and health clubs?

6. Should women have the same freedom in meeting and dating men as men have with regard to women? Explain.

7. Is jealousy good or bad? Explain.

Review: Discussion as Argument: Approaches

How many approaches to "discussion as argument" can you remember and describe? Only after you have checked your memory completely should you refer to the information at the end of chapter 11.

1. _____
   _____
   _____
   _____

2. _____
   _____
   _____
   _____

3. _____
   _____
   _____
   _____

Exercise 8—Presentations: Roles of the Sexes

The Case of the Green Eyes, or "Isle Be Seeing You" and the discussion exercise dealt largely with the relationship between men and women, specifically the love relationship. That focus can be expanded to look at the lives of men and women much more fully. Make a five-to-seven-minute presentation about one of the following topics as it relates to the lives of men and women in your native country or culture.

Numbers 1 to 3 are general and 4 to 8 are somewhat more specific. For any number, narrow the subject so that it will not be too large or too general for your time and purpose.

Remember to (1) carefully plan and organize your presentation, (2) use specific language, (3) offer visual aids if appropriate and helpful, and (4) support your speaking with body language. Also, study the information below about attention-getters; it will help you to prepare for your presentation.

Presentation Topics

1. Traditional roles for men and women

2. Changes in roles for men and women

3. Roles for men and women that you would like to see in the future

4. Educational and job opportunities for men and women

5. Rights and political power of men and women

6. Family responsibilities for men and women

7. Decision making between men and women

8. Freedom of activity for men and women socially

Attention-Getters in Presentations

The most important part of a presentation is the beginning. If it does not create interest or get attention, then there is the danger of losing an audience either figuratively or literally. The kind of beginning you will use for a presentation will depend on the total situation, including your subject, your purpose, and the kind of audience present. In general, however, there are a variety of attention-getters that are useful in getting attention and making a good beginning. They are listed here.

1. Give an interesting, a surprising, or in some cases even a funny detail about your subject.

2. Tell a short anecdote (story) that relates to your subject and serves to illustrate it in some way.

3. Address all the members of the audience directly, especially to describe an experience they are likely to have had in relation to your subject.

4. Ask the audience a specific question related to your subject and then answer the question.

5. Filter your subject through your personal perspective or experience—immediately personalize the subject. But do not emphasize yourself over your subject. Instead, create a sense of shared human experience.

Consider an attention-getter from each of these possibilities and develop one for your presentation. Practice using attention-getters appropriately in other presentations that you give.

13 A Case of Spirits

Prelistening: The Situation

In this case, Sherlock Holmes is confronted not with a problem of the heart, as in the preceding case, but with a problem of the mind—or even a problem of the spirit! That is to say, the person who comes to him for help is troubled in both mind and spirit because he has been troubled with spirits. The "spirits" in this case do not change in shape or appearance, but in kind. Holmes's job is to recognize the different kinds of "spirits" and, once again, to deal with the hard facts, not with the supernatural.

Instructions

1. Listen to the taped account of the case in order to get a general understanding of it. Then listen again, read the notes about the case as you listen, and fill in the blank spaces. You may use exact words from the tape for some blanks, but for others you should summarize or paraphrase. You may also want to use abbreviations so that you can more easily keep up with the tape.

2. After you finish listening and filling in the blanks, answer the questions that follow.

Case Notes

Visitor wants _____!
    After _____, went to Casey's _____
      Drank several _____
    Left _____—met _____
      Told spirit to _____
      Bet spirit it _____
    Ran away from _____—but it _____
      Along _____ downtown
  Holmes's advice— _____
    Because _____

Questions

Answer these questions orally or in writing.

1. How would you describe the general condition of Holmes's visitor?

2. What did the man do when he got out of work this evening?

3. How much did he drink?

4. What did he come across after he left the bar?

5. What did he tell the thing that he met?

6. What "mistake" did he then make?

7. What happened when he ran away from the thing?

8. Where were they running?

9. How does Holmes know where they were running? Why does he tell the man to take a good look at one of the store windows?

10. Can you solve this mystery with Holmes by completing his words at the end?

11. Why is the title of the story appropriate?

12. What do you notice about Holmes as a listener in this case—what does he do? Why do you think he does this? (Consider the expression, "You took the words right out of my mouth.")

Listening Skill: Anticipating

In *A Case of Spirits*, Sherlock Holmes anticipated his visitor's words several times. The listening skill of *anticipating* is a lot like inferring. It is listening and thinking carefully at the same time, but instead of making a thoughtful conclusion about a completed, indirect message, the listener makes a conclusion about an incomplete message. As a matter of fact, the listener actually concludes the message before he or she hears the end of it. As with inferring, this process may not occur as naturally or as quickly when a second language is involved because we may be concentrating very hard on hearing actual spoken words and on understanding their direct meanings. It may seem that we have little time or energy to think ahead with the speaker.

Practicing and improving anticipation will greatly improve listening comprehension and overall conversation ability. There are several things that make practice possible. First, it is a fact that we can listen and think about four times faster than someone can speak. The average speaker speaks approximately 125 words per minute. We can listen and think at a rate of 500 words per minute. Therefore, we can and should make more use of this greater speed and the time it gives us.

We can also improve our ability to anticipate or predict meanings by becoming more aware of redundancy in language. *Redundancy* means that we have more than one source of information for anticipating the word or words that will be spoken or the message that will be expressed. For example, listen to the following statement and try to anticipate how it will end. Fill in the blank spaces.

Statement	Possible Response
It's amazing. You know what I'm going to _____ before I even . . .	_____

Quite possibly you did not even need the extra *aural information* of hearing the sound /s/ after "even" in order to complete the speaker's thought. The *grammatical information* of object following subject and verb, as in "You know" and then "what I'm going to say," may have helped you to know that the next words after "I even" would be another verb and object. The incomplete dependent clause "before I even" and the usual substitution of a pronoun for an already stated object ("it" for "what I'm going to say") were probably additional helps. The *semantic information*, which is the meaning of words, may have been the greatest help of all. The words "know," "what I'm going to say" (I haven't said it yet), and especially the word "before" gave the idea that you would know in advance the end of the speaker's message.

Anticipating, like inferring, is an advanced listening skill. You think along with the speaker and help to complete his or her thought. Sometimes you will do this aloud to help the speaker conclude a thought, especially if he or she pauses or stops, or if you want to show how well you are listening and thinking along. This will aid the conversation and the communication between you. You will not, of course, want to interrupt impolitely when the speaker is completely capable and desirous of completing his or her idea. Most of the time you will anticipate silently to yourself and then hear if you have anticipated correctly. In all cases, your mind will not be a blank. You will be active in your listening and prepared to understand and respond—communication will be on a high level.

Exercise 1—Anticipating: Aural Information, I

Listen to the statements on the tape, fill in the blank spaces as you listen, and try to anticipate the speaker's end word or words. Aural information will be provided to help you.

1. _____ are my favorite _____ at the _____.

2. I'm glad that I don't have any _____ on Friday _____.

3. Many people don't have time in the _____ for _____.

4. Their little _____ is very _____.

5. _____ one _____ at a time and _____ look _____.

6. Jae Kon needs to get his _____ _____.

7. Martha had to _____ home because of an _____.

8. It's time to take the _____ out of the _____.

9. _____ here—that _____ over there is _____.

10. There are many ways to _____ to your _____.

11. Mrs. Soto's _____ told her to _____ _____.

12. They _____ three nights a week in the _____.

13. It's really _____ hard. Can I borrow your _____?

14. It's impossible to get a _____ at some _____ without a _____.

15. People used to consider the idea of traveling in _____ to be _____.

Exercise 2—Anticipating: Aural Information, II

Aural information may take many different forms. In the following song, the need for rhymes will help you to anticipate the unspoken parts. Fill in the missing words as well as the unspoken parts as you listen to the tape.

I'm being _____ by a boa constrictor,
I'm being _____ by a boa constrictor,
I'm being _____ by a boa constrictor,
And I don't _____ it very much.
O _____, O _____, he's _____ to my
_____ — _____ to my _____!
O _____, O _____, he's _____ to my
_____ — _____ to my _____!
O _____, O _____, he's _____ to my
_____ — _____ to my _____!
O _____, O _____, he's _____ to my
_____ — _____ to my _____!
O _____, O _____, he's _____ to my
_____!

Exercise 3—Anticipating: Grammatical Information

Listen to the statements on the tape, fill in the blank spaces as you listen, and try to anticipate the speaker's end word or words. Grammatical information will be an important aid in this exercise.

1. I _____ for it, so it belongs _____ .

2. They started _____ apples at 9:00, and they've _____ over 300 _____ .

3. You have a simple choice for this _____—either you _____ hard or _____ .

4. Chicago is a _____ city, but New York _____ .

5. Naoko, I would find a _____ place to _____ if I _____ .

6. He _____ the new best-selling book from the _____ instead of going to a _____ and _____ .

7. The _____ she tried, the _____ _____ .

8. We don't want to buy _____ the package—we only want _____ .

9. Toi Yee didn't feel _____ during the performance, _____ she felt _____ .

10. A _____ dealer cheated _____ once in my _____ , and no other _____ _____ _____ .

11. Like most people, I go to the _____ to _____ and _____ .

12. Khalil would rather _____ late than _____ .

13. There is a lot of _____ with _____ son or daughter, and with _____ _____ .

14. He talks _____ , but he thinks _____ .

15. Ok Sil works a lot of extra hours as a _____ , so naturally she saw the _____ while _____ .

Exercise 4—Anticipating: Semantic Information, I

Aural information and grammatical information were very important to anticipating in the previous three exercises, but so was semantic information. These sources of information are closely connected. Semantic information will be especially important in this exercise since anticipation of the general message, rather than anticipation of a specific word or words, is called for. It should also be mentioned that anticipating from semantic information relies upon the meanings of words in the spoken context, but it also draws upon a listener's knowledge of related meanings in a culture or in the world as a whole.

Listen to the statements on the tape, fill in the blank spaces as you listen, and try to anticipate the speakers' messages. The first one is done for you as an example.

1. The important thing about *education* is not just *getting* it. What's really important is *doing something with it.*

2. _____ won't create great problems with _____ because we will always need _____ to

_____

3. Akira jokes about drinking _____. He calls it "_____ _____." After he has had a _____, he

_____

4. It is often difficult to accept the _____ of a _____ one. Even weeks or months afterwards, it's common for a person to _____ that

_____

5. Some restaurants have _____ about the way customers should _____. For example, I tried going into one place with a _____ but no _____, and _____

6. The idea of a human being _____ completely under his or her own _____ was once a _____, and then it seemed an _____. But a few years ago _____

7. House _____ can fool you sometimes. It might seem that they're _____ or even completely _____, but then _____

8. When people think of _____, they usually think of _____ against _____ people. Well, the most challenging and meaningful _____ is really _____

9. I paid $125 to get _____ ready for the winter. So, what happened? I ran out to _____ this morning to _____, and _____

10. _____ are very interesting. Sometimes you don't know if they _____ what you _____ them—like a new _____, for example. Then, two or three days later _____

Exercise 5—Anticipating: Semantic Information, II

Listen to the statements on the tape and try to anticipate the speakers' messages. Write your answers on the lines provided. The first one is done for you as an example.

1. *want to eat at home (cook their own food, etc)*

2. _____

3. _____

4. _____

5. _____

6. _____

7. _____

8. _____

9. _____

10. _____

Exercise 6—Anticipating from Student Statements

On the lines below, plan some statements for which your classmates will have to anticipate the final message. Make sure that you provide enough information for them to be able to anticipate. People's efforts to anticipate are not always successful; if your classmates do not understand your meaning immediately, simply help them as you would in a regular conversation.

1. _____
   _____
   _____

2. _____
   _____
   _____

3. _____
   _____
   _____

Exercise 7—The Effect of Culture on Inferring and Anticipating

There are many factors that affect inferring and anticipating. As we have seen with anticipating, the sounds of words, grammar or syntax, and the meanings of words all play a part. Cultural and world knowledge are also very important, as exercise 4 briefly noted. For example, number 2 in exercise 4 referred to a concern that machines may replace people in jobs and thus cause problems with unemployment. If a person comes from a culture in which that concern is not a reality—it has not been expressed or discussed very much, if at all—then it becomes difficult to infer or anticipate in a context in which it is a concern.

Examine all of the statements in exercise 4. Note any information that, with respect to your cultural background, might make the statements difficult for you to infer or to anticipate from. Compare your notes with those of other students.

1. _____
   _____
2. _____
   _____
3. _____
   _____
4. _____
   _____
5. _____
   _____

Exercise 8—The Effect of Idioms on Inferring and Anticipating

Another factor that can affect one's ability to infer or to anticipate—or that can affect understanding itself—is the presence of idioms. In chapter 8, you studied how to guess the meanings of idioms and how to ask for an explanation if you could not guess the meaning. The category of idioms known as two-word verbs sometimes poses a special problem because these idioms do not stand out easily and thus may not be recognized—they are shorter and less colorful than many other idioms. *A Case of Spirits* contained many of these two-word verbs, which consist of a verb plus a preposition or even of a verb plus two prepositions, resulting in a "three-word verb."

With other students in a small group, make a list of all the two-word and three-word verbs that you can find in *A Case of Spirits*. Also, write an original sentence using each verb. The first one is done for you as an example.

1. bring up—I brought your mail up.
2. _____
3. _____
4. _____
5. _____
6. _____
7. _____
8. _____
9. _____
10. _____

11. _____

12. _____

13. _____

14. _____

15. _____

16. _____

17. _____

18. _____

There are two categories of two-word verbs: *separable* and *inseparable. Separable two-word verbs* can be separated by noun objects, and they must be separated by pronoun objects.

> Example: She *made up* that story.
> (invented)
> She *made* that story *up.*
> She *made* it *up.*

Inseparable two-word verbs can never be separated by an object.

> Example: Please *go over* your mistakes.
> (review)
> Please *go over* them.

Examine the two-word verbs in your list above, determine which ones can be separated, and put a * next to those. Share your list of verbs, your sentences, and your determinations about separability in class. Make all of these two-word verbs and the ones in chapter 8 part of your vocabulary.

Exercise 9—Discussion: Spirits

The visitor in *A Case of Spirits* certainly had a problem with "spirits." He had to drink alcohol to get into a holiday spirit, then he drank too many spirits (alcohol), and that resulted in his thinking that he saw a spirit. Read the following discussion questions about "spirits" and choose one or more to talk about. Before you begin discussing them, however, study the information on the next page about "participant orientations" so that you will be able to understand and function well as a discussion participant.

Discussion Questions

1. What does "holiday spirit" mean to you? Give examples from your native culture.

2. Has any holiday in your native culture changed in spirit to some extent? Does the original spirit continue in large or small part? Explain.

3. What is your opinion of people who drink alcohol (not necessarily a lot) as a way of celebrating a holiday?

4. How big a problem is alcoholism or drug abuse in your native country? How seriously do people view these abuse problems? What public measures are taken to deal with these problems?

5. In some countries, drug abuse is looked upon and treated more seriously than alcoholism is. Do you agree or disagree with this difference? Explain.

6. Why do you think human beings first created and continue to use such things as alcohol and escapist drugs?

7. Do you believe in spirits, some kinds of ghosts, on earth? Explain.

8. What would you do if you ever saw a ghost?

Participant Orientations in Discussions

Understanding the roles that you can play in group discussions can help you improve your participation in them. It can also help you improve your overall ability to listen, think, and speak in English. You can start by considering three categories of roles: (1) participant, (2) leader, and (3) nonparticipant. The participant category, which may be considered the broadest, is described below (the leader and nonparticipant categories are discussed in chapter 15). It, too, may be separated into three categories.

1. *Task-oriented Participant:* This kind of participant is dedicated to accomplishing whatever task or work that the group faces. The feelings of individual group members or of the group as a whole are not of concern to this participant.

2. *Relational-oriented Participant:* This kind of participant is concerned with individual and group feelings. Making everyone feel a part of the group and a part of the group's decision-making process is important in this orientation.

3. *Self-oriented Participant:* This kind of participant is more concerned with himself or herself than with the group or the group's task. This person may have a difficult time escaping a sense of nervousness or self-consciousness. He or she may be overly accepting of others' opinions in order to avoid conflict or trouble. The opposite tendency, to be overly unaccepting of others' opinions, may also characterize this person. Too much of a joking attitude may also reflect the person's insecurity or desire for ego fulfillment. Too much self-relating—relating everything in the discussion to oneself—may also detract from the work of the group and ignore the feelings of others.

Although a self-oriented participation may seem more negative than the others, it should not be understood in that way. This is a natural way to be, and it would only be a problem if it were manifested in the extreme. After all, relating ideas to oneself or to one's own experience can be beneficial. Similarly, a relational-oriented or a task-oriented participation manifested in the extreme would also cause problems. Usually, people will possess different orientations at different times in a discussion, and shifts from one to another will occur. The overall matter for review is this: which is your general orientation?

Be aware of your orientation as you participate in the discussion activity above and as you participate in other discussions in the future. You may decide as you proceed in a discussion that it would be helpful to shift orientations at some points, perhaps becoming more relational-oriented at one time and more task-oriented at another time. After the class discussion, you and your classmates may improve your awareness and future participation by sharing perceptions about one another's orientations.

14 The Case of the Cheap Déjà Vu

Prelistening: The Situation

In this case, Professor Fulton Flake presents Sherlock Holmes with another problem of the mind—perhaps a problem of two minds!—or two problems of the same mind! On the one hand, the professor seems to sense too little, and on the other hand, he seems to sense too much. Is the professor in fact "losing his senses"? And can Holmes "make sense" of the whole mess? Join him in solving *The Case of the Cheap Déjà Vu!*

Instructions

1. There are eight sections in the taped account of this case. There will be time after each section for you to anticipate the end message of statements begun by Holmes's visitor, Professor Flake. Write your anticipations as quickly as you can on the numbered lines below.

2. After you have had time for anticipating, you will hear Holmes's own anticipations. Compare your anticipations with his to see if you have the same general meaning; you do not need to have the same words.

Anticipations for the Eight Sections

1. _____

2. _____

3. _____

4. _____

5. _____

6. _____

7. _____

8. _____

Questions

Answer these questions orally or in writing.

1. What are the two parts to Professor Flake's problem?

2. Who should solve this problem, according to Holmes? Why do you think he says this?

3. What does Holmes believe is a cause of the Professor's problem?

4. What is the one thing that Professor Flake does not forget about, according to his wife?

5. Does Professor Flake seem to have a déjà vu experience while talking with Holmes? Explain.

6. Why is the experience really not a case of déjà vu? Solve the mystery with Holmes by completing his message at the end.

7. How is the Professor's sense of déjà vu connected in general with his forgetfulness?

8. How do Holmes and Profesor Flake differ with regard to how much the Professor should pay Holmes for his services? How is the Professor "forgetful" with regard to money in this situation?

9. Why does Holmes complete so many of the Professor's statements? Why does Holmes then want the Professor to complete Holmes's own statement at the end?

10. Why is the title of the story appropriate?

Listening Skill: More about Inferring and Anticipating

In *The Case of the Cheap Déjà Vu*, important communication occurred between Sherlock Holmes and Professor Flake through the use of spoken emphasis. Words were emphasized as a way of implying messages for the listener to infer or anticipate. Here are the two major examples of spoken emphasis from Holmes: the emphasized words are underlined.

1. "And what if you actually <u>had</u> been here yesterday and we actually <u>had</u> done all this before?"

2. "Forget it? Let it go by? Sorry, Professor, <u>I</u> cannot. Especially since this is not the <u>second</u> time you've been here, but <u>actually</u> . . .

In the first example, *had* is emphasized twice to imply very strongly that the Professor had indeed visited the day before. In the second example, *I* is emphasized because Holmes recognizes that the professor would purposely like to forget about paying for more than one visit. *Second* is emphasized to call attention to the fact that there has been more than one visit, and *actually* is emphasized to propel or force the professor to complete the message with the actual number of visits. The use of *actually*, an emphatic word in itself, in both examples, also contributes to the force of meaning.

Emphasis is an important factor in inferring and anticipating. It is the factor that you will become more aware of and practice working with in the first two exercises below. Other factors will be covered in the succeeding exercises.

Exercise 1—Recognizing and Using Emphasis for Meaning

Look at the sentence that appears five times below and listen to the five different ways it is spoken on the tape. Underline the word that is emphasized each time and quickly note the effect on the meaning. Discuss these effects in class. Also, practice imitating the different emphases.

1. Mary swam across the river.
Effect on meaning: _____
_____

2. Mary swam across the river.
Effect on meaning: _____
_____

3. Mary swam across the river.
Effect on meaning: _____
_____

4. Mary swam across the river.
Effect on meaning: _____
_____

5. Mary swam across the river.
Effect on meaning: _____
_____

Exercise 2—Student Emphases

Your teacher will assign you one of the sentences below and one part of that sentence to emphasize. He or she will make similar assignments to other students. After a short practice, you and your classmates will demonstrate emphasizing the different parts of these sentences. Discuss the effects on meaning.

1. Anita wrote a feature for the city newspaper.

2. Martin baked some cheesecake cookies for his class.

3. Classes will end at noon this Thursday.

4. Dancing in the shower is almost unheard of.

5. The smallest woman in our karate class proved to be the best fighter.

Exercise 3—Recognizing Attitudes and Their Effects on Meaning

We use our voices to communicate many different things. Listen to the tape and note the different ways that the simple sentence, "Mary swam across the river," can be said with regard to attitude. On the lines below briefly state the attitudes that are expressed and their effects on meaning. The first one is done for you as an example.

1. Attitude: **Unbelieving**
Effect on meaning: *It's doubtful that she did it.*

2. Attitude: _____
Effect on meaning: _____
_____

3. Attitude: _____
Effect on meaning: _____
_____

4. Attitude: _____
Effect on meaning: _____
_____

5. Attitude: _____
Effect on meaning: _____
_____

Exercise 4—Student Attitudes

Plan and practice expressing a different attitude for each of the sentences in exercise 2. Present your ways of expressing the sentences and listen to the other students' ways. Identify one another's attitudes and discuss how they affect the meaning of the sentences.

1. Attitude: _____
2. Attitude: _____
3. Attitude: _____
4. Attitude: _____
5. Attitude: _____

Exercise 5—More Student Attitudes

On the lines below, write a sentence of your own and plan three different attitudes for expressing the sentence. Consider many different possibilities: envy, joy, disappointment, pride, enthusiasm, disgust, and so on. Then present the three different ways of expressing your sentence and listen to the other students do the same with their sentences. Identify one another's attitudes and discuss their effects on meaning.

Your sentence: _____

_____

Attitude 1: _____

Attitude 2: _____

Attitude 3: _____

Exercise 6—Cultural and Individual Anticipations

Cultural identity and experience play an important part in whether we can anticipate in a particular spoken context and also in how we anticipate. Individual identity and experience play a similar part. These "identities" and experiences are behind the anticipations, expectations, or even promises that we feel with regard to life in general. The sight of birds flying south is a promise of the approach of winter for some people. Sneezing, a runny nose, and a scratchy throat might "promise" that a person is catching a cold. Listen to the things mentioned on the tape and write the promise that each holds for you. Also note why you thought of that promise. Compare your responses in class.

1. Promise: _____
Why that promise? _____

2. Promise: _____
Why? _____

3. Promise: _____
Why? _____

4. Promise: _____
Why? _____

5. Promise: _____
Why? _____

6. Promise: _____
Why? _____

7. Promise: _____
Why? _____

8. Promise: _____
Why? _____

9. Promise: _____
Why? _____

10. Promise: _____
Why? _____

Exercise 7—Student Promises

Imagine that you could make fantastic changes in the world and what the results of those changes would be. Answer the questions below and use the "If I could . . . , then . . ." structure as a guide. The first one is done for you as an example. When you are finished, share the "if" part of some of your sentences with your classmates, and they will try to anticipate the "then" part— the promise part.

1. What would you make talk?
If I could make *animals talk*_____,
then *we could find out what they think about us*.

2. What would you make faster?
If I could make _____,
then _____.

3. What would you make softer?
If I could make _____,
then _____.

4. What would you make invisible?
If I could make _____,
then _____.

5. What would you make edible?
If I could make _____,
then _____.

6. What would you make sweeter?
If I could make _____,
then _____.

7. What would you make red?
If I could make _____,
then _____.

8. What would you make quieter?
If I could make _____,
then _____.

9. What would you make new?
If I could make _____,
then _____.

10. What would you turn into gold?
If I could turn _____,
then _____.

Exercise 8—Discussion: Work

In *The Case of the Cheap Déjà Vu*, Sherlock Holmes and Professor Flake identified the Professor's overinvolvement in his work as contributing to his problem with forgetfulness. There is perhaps no bigger subject than the role of work in people's lives. Read the following discussion questions about work and choose one or more to talk about. First, though, test your memory of the different kinds of "participant orientations" in a discussion. Describe them in the review section on the next page. Review these orientations in order to help yourself understand and function well in the discussion activity.

Discussion Questions

1. How important a role does work play in a person's life?

2. What are the most important things that work should give a person? List them in order of importance.

3. What would you consider to be the ideal kind of work?

4. Which would be better—a life of complete leisure or a life with satisfying work? Why?

5. Which do you believe is more important in a job—security or the possibility for advancement? Why?

6. In some cultures, it is common for people to be with the same employer for their entire working life. In other cultures, it is common for people to be with several employers during their working life. What are the advantages and disadvantages of these two situations?

7. Compare several common jobs in a society with regard to how much they are valued in terms of both money and respect. Do you agree with the way these jobs are valued, or do you believe that some should be valued more—or less—highly than they are? Explain the reasons for your beliefs. (The values assigned, of course, may be different in different cultures.)

8. How serious a problem do you think it is to be a workaholic?

Review: Participant Orientations in Discussions

How many kinds of "participant orientations" can you remember and describe? Only after you have checked your memory completely should you refer to the information at the end of chapter 13.

Participant Orientations

1. _____
   _____
   _____
   _____

2. _____
   _____
   _____
   _____

3. _____
   _____
   _____
   _____

Exercise 9—Presentations: A Memory

Forgetting and remembering were the key elements in *The Case of the Cheap Déjà Vu*. Remembering from one day to the next and from one year to another plays an important part in general in shaping our lives. Often there are a few particular memories that are especially important to us. They may be funny or sad, joyous or bitter, but they stay with us mainly because they were meaningful in some important way. Pick one of your own memories of an experience in which you learned something important; tell the class about it, and explain the meaning it holds for you.

Remember to (1) carefully plan and organize your presentation, (2) use specific language, (3) offer visual aids if appropriate and helpful, (4) support your speaking with body language, and (5) use an appropriate attention-getter. Also, study the information below about the voice; it will further help you to prepare for your presentation.

The Voice in Presentations

Your *voice* itself is potentially one of your most effective means of communicating your ideas, of emphasizing certain of those ideas, and of creating and keeping interest. In this chapter we have focused on the emphases, attitudes, and meanings that can be expressed by changing or varying speech patterns. In the extended speaking that you do in a presentation, using your voice meaningfully is especially important. It is commonly said in English-speaking contexts that there is nothing worse than listening to a speaker whose voice is flat and expressionless—a monotone.

The use of the voice is, of course, very individual, and it depends greatly on your subject, purpose, and audience. The possibilities for using your voice may be especially great when you are telling about a particular personal experience, as in this exercise. Here are some common uses of the voice to consider.

1. *Slowing the voice, and/or lowering the tone:* This is often used for emphasis—for something important, for something serious; this way of speaking may also be more definite and more distinct.

2. *Speaking more quietly, or possibly more loudly:* This change may also be used for emphasis; it may be used with number 1 for even greater effect.

3. *Speaking faster, possibly in a higher tone and with more volume*: This variation may be used for telling about an action, about something exciting, or about something light or humorous.

4. *Attitude inflection*: This shows attitude in your voice—your feeling about what you are saying—as discussed earlier in this chapter.

5. *Character inflection*: This gives a sense of different people, of different speakers, especially when telling an anecdote or a longer story; this does not require great acting ability!

Consider these possibilities, try using some of them, or think of others that may fit you and your presentation, above. Using your voice in different ways may appear difficult to you at first, and it may even cause you some discomfort. But with practice it will most likely prove to be liberating—a new source of comfort and command as you gain a sense of greater expressiveness in English.

15 The Case of Life or Death

Prelistening: The Situation

Unlike the previous cases, this case does not involve an updated version of Sherlock Holmes. Instead, it involves a descendant of his in the far distant future. Sherlock Holmes XIII does not even bear the title "detective." It is true that he uses the same mental powers as the original Holmes, but he uses them to solve mysteries of far greater importance in a far greater region— the entire universe. That is why he is called "The Great Cosmic Unraveler." And no greater mystery or question has ever confronted him than the present one, on the planet Htrae, inhabited by a people called the Oge Retla. The question that he seeks to answer in this futuristic science-fiction story is the timeless one of—life or death?

Instructions

1. Listen to the taped account of the case in order to get a general understanding of it. Then, as you listen again, take your own notes in the space provided below.

2. After you finish listening and taking notes, answer the questions that follow.

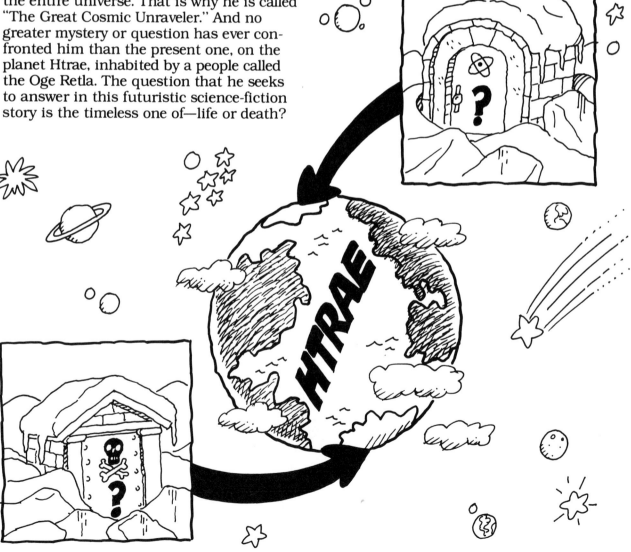

Case Notes

Questions

Answer these questions orally or in writing.

1. What year is it in this science-fiction story?

2. Who is Sherlock Holmes XIII, and what has he done?

3. What has happened to the Oge Retla on the planet Htrae?

4. Were the Oge Retla the original inhabitants of Htrae? Explain.

5. In what ways were the Oge Retla similar to the Earth people?

6. What kind of historical perspective did the Oge Retla have?

7. How would you compare the Oge Retla's emotional development with their intellectual development?

8. In their last days, what was the attitude of the Oge Retla toward the Earth people and the future?

9. What did the Oge Retla leave behind them in two great vaults?

10. What message did they also leave behind?

11. What mystery or problem does Holmes XIII have to solve? How can he solve it with only the information that is available in the story?

12. Would you open the north-pole vault or the south-pole vault? Explain your choice.

13. What are Htrae and Oge Retla spelled backwards? Why are these appropriate names in the story?

Listening Skill: Evaluating

Evaluating is an advanced listening skill that involves careful thinking. It can be compared with inferring and anticipating as skills that involve judgment. With inferring, we try to judge the real message of a communication. With anticipating, we try to judge the outcome or end part of a communication before we receive all of it. With *evaluating*, which contains the word "value," we try to judge the value or worth of a communication. Is the communication true, right, or good? Is it something we agree or disagree with?

In *The Case of Life or Death*, Holmes XIII— and we—have to evaluate the Oge Retla's message about opening the north pole vault. Does that vault contain life or death? And how can we judge? What is the best judgment possible? It is a difficult case, very difficult to judge, but we make our best judgment based on the information we have in the story.

Our evaluating is often based on information or criteria that are given to us, either wholly or partly, as in *The Case of Life or Death*. That is, our judgment is still our own, but it is based on criteria wholly or partly outside ourselves. At other times, our evaluating will be based more heavily on criteria that we determine for ourselves. Listen to the example on the tape and fill in the blank spaces below as you listen.

Statement

Shoplifting isn't so _____ if you really _____ something— like something for your _____ —and you don't have the _____ for it. After all, you're _____ from a big _____, not an individual, and big businesses do their own kind of _____ from us all the time.

Possible Responses

1. Well, that may be what _____ think. For _____, it's still _____, which is _____ in any situation.

2. I see what you're saying, but _____ like that can still end up _____ someone — _____ getting less _____ because of smaller _____, other consumers _____ more for things for the same reason, even _____ yourself because of the way you end up _____ about yourself.

3. I _____ with you, but only in very special _____.

These are just three of many possible responses, all based on individually determined criteria.

The evaluating response may take the form of expressing an opinion, agreeing, disagreeing, or deciding on an action, all similar to what you have experienced in discussions. The important thing to be aware of is the basis, the criteria, for evaluating. Sometimes the criteria will be wholly or partly given, as in *The Case of Life or Death*, and sometimes they will be more personal, as in the conversation about shoplifting, above.

There are many situations in which we will do our evaluating silently to ourselves. For example, there may simply be no opportunity to respond aloud, or we may feel that the subject is too sensitive to respond to openly. At other times, however, a spoken response can aid the evaluating process by making us more aware of how we think and what we value. Also, it can improve communication and under-standing between people.

As with the other listening skills you have studied, practiced, and learned, evaluating can help you improve your ability to operate in English. And like inferring and antici-pating in particular, it is further proof that literal comprehension alone is not enough for good listening ability. It is often necessary to evaluate at the same time that you listen; otherwise, there may be insufficient understanding or even worse consequences. For example, imagine you were part of the conversation about shoplifting, above, and consider what might happen if you failed to evaluate from your own personal criteria.

Exercise 1—Ethical Evaluating, I

You will hear a series of statements on the tape that deal with ethics—with what is the right or wrong, acceptable or unacceptable, conduct in different situations. Fill in the blanks as you listen and evaluate the statements according to *your own criteria*. Write your responses on the lines provided. The first one is done for you as an example. After you are finished, you might compare responses in class (there are good possibilities for discussion).

1. It's a person's responsibility to **report** anyone that he or she sees *Shoplifting*.
Response: *I wouldn't say "anyone"—different factors would influence my decision about reporting someone or not.*

2. Some people on the streets in big cities ＿＿＿＿ "spare change," like twenty-five cents. It's a ＿＿ idea to ＿＿ it to them if you ＿＿.
Response: ＿＿＿＿＿＿＿＿＿＿
＿＿＿＿＿＿＿＿＿＿＿
＿＿＿＿＿＿＿＿＿＿＿
＿＿＿＿＿＿＿＿＿＿＿

3. If there's a ＿＿ of people waiting for something and you're in too much of a ＿＿ to go to the ＿＿ of the line, it's okay to go to the ＿＿ the other people.
Response: ＿＿＿＿＿＿＿＿＿
＿＿＿＿＿＿＿＿＿＿＿
＿＿＿＿＿＿＿＿＿＿＿
＿＿＿＿＿＿＿＿＿＿＿

4. It's not right to ＿＿＿ about one friend to another friend, or to ＿＿＿ one co-worker in a conversation you're having with another co-worker.
Response: ＿＿＿＿＿＿＿＿＿
＿＿＿＿＿＿＿＿＿＿＿
＿＿＿＿＿＿＿＿＿＿＿
＿＿＿＿＿＿＿＿＿＿＿

5. If you really need the ＿＿, it's okay to have ＿＿＿ do your ＿＿＿ for you.
Response: ＿＿＿＿＿＿＿＿＿
＿＿＿＿＿＿＿＿＿＿＿
＿＿＿＿＿＿＿＿＿＿＿
＿＿＿＿＿＿＿＿＿＿＿

6. There's nothing wrong with _____ at someone who makes a really _____ .
Response: _____
_____
_____
_____

7. If your _____ give you some _____ advice, you should tell them so, just as you would tell _____ else.
Response: _____
_____
_____
_____

8. If a classmate wants to _____ in school, that's his or her _____ as long as he or she doesn't try to _____ from you.
Response: _____
_____
_____
_____

9. If a cashier in a store gives you back _____ change and you _____ it, that's not _____—that's just his or her _____ .
Response: _____
_____
_____
_____

10. Being _____ to someone only because you _____ something from him or her is understood and acceptable _____ .
Response: _____
_____
_____
_____

Exercise 2—Ethical Evaluating, II

You will hear more statements on tape dealing with ethics. Listen carefully and evaluate the statements according to *your own criteria.* Write only your responses on the lines provided. After you are finished, compare responses in class.

1. _____
_____

2. _____
_____

3. _____
_____

4. _____
_____

5. _____
_____

6. _____
_____

7. _____
_____

8. _____
_____

9. _____
_____

10. _____
_____

Exercise 3—Student Ethical Statements

Use the topics below to plan ethical statements of your own that your classmates will have to evaluate. Make sure that your statements are the kind that the students will have to evaluate carefully. It may be helpful to plan your statements in writing before telling them to the class.

1. Playing music loudly: _____
   _____
   _____

2. Talking in the library: _____
   _____
   _____

3. Helping unfortunate people: _____
   _____
   _____

4. Paying bills on time: _____
   _____
   _____

5. Borrowing: _____
   _____
   _____

6. Leaving tips in restaurants: _____
   _____
   _____

7. Getting to class late: _____
   _____
   _____

8. Littering: _____
   _____
   _____

9. Swearing (using offensive words): _____
   _____
   _____

10. Caring about yourself first: _____
    _____
    _____

11. Arguing with parents: _____
    _____
    _____

12. Writing graffiti: _____
    _____
    _____

13. Smoking in public places: _____
    _____
    _____

14. Drinking alcohol: _____
    _____
    _____

15. Doing your best: _____
    _____
    _____

Exercise 4—Evaluating Advertising Statements

Advertising can be helpful because it is informative. It can also be manipulative because it is persuasive. It attempts to influence our abilty to evaluate—that is, our ability to judge the worth or value of something in order to decide whether or not we want to spend our money on it. It may also be said that advertising often tries to increase our sense of the value of something without providing reasonable support, or that it tries to slip outside criteria into our personal criteria. Its criteria are usually more emotional than logical.

It is possible to evaluate advertising statements themselves with regard to how they attempt to influence our ability to think or to evaluate reasonably. Study the advertising techniques below and discuss how the examples work. Then listen to the advertising statements on the tape, and evaluate those statements in terms of the techniques they use.

1. *Weasel Words*: Like the sly weasel that sneaks into a chicken coop and sucks out the insides of eggs, weasel words are those words that sneak into our minds and steal from our rationality in order to sell us

something. They include words like "help," "can," "like," "virtually," "work on," and "act on." None of those words means that there *will* be a specific positive result connected with a product or service—but we are led to think so.

Examples: Healthmint mouthwash *can* (or *helps*) keep the common cold from catching you.

Sipping Venal wine is *like* spending a romantic evening on a Venetian gondola.

2. *Buzz Words*: Buzz words are words (and ideas) that are very popular. They are picked up by the advertising world and used to promote greater sales. Anything to do with physical fitness fits this category these days in the United States. Much older, but still used, are buzz words that relate to natural things, like the word "natural" itself, "lemon," and other fruits or plants.

Example: Shimmer shampoo with *aloe* brightens both your days and nights.

3. *Subjective Opinion:* Any business has the right to express the personal opinion that its product or service is the best. It can do that even though there is no way to prove that it really is the best or because there is no way to prove it. The product or service is most likely about the same as others of its kind. The Subjective Opinion technique especially applies to matters of taste (in the sense of liking something or not), which is, of course, very subjective.

Example: Venal grapes are naturally *the best.*

4. *Questionable Authority:* This involves a famous person expressing an opinion or recommending an action in an area in which he or she has no special knowledge or expertise.

Example: Frank Sinatra recommends Starpitch as the ultimate sing-along machine, the car that's virtually never out of tune.

5. *Bandwagon:* Because so many others share the same opinion or are doing something (buying something), you should too. This is not a logical conclusion.

Example: Sixty million Frenchmen can't be wrong—Clouzot cologne for men has just the right touch for women everywhere.

6. *Testimonials by Everyday People:* This usually involves a person's testing or comparing two or more similar products. Advertisers will interview as many people as necessary and through media influence and financial reward get just the right spokesperson for their product or service. This "everyman" approach is related to 4 and 5, above.

Example: Policeman Joe Badge knows all about dirty hands as well as about the long arm of the law. He has compared the leading bars of soap, and it's new, improved Pure-All that comes clean with him.

7. *Use of Statistics:* An advertiser will use statistics to serve its own interests. Any "survey" it reports will most likely be limited to the very small number of people who give the kind of response that it wants.

Example: Three out of four auto mechanics recommend Zoom gasoline for that racing feeling.

8. *Emotional Appeals in General:* These may include, for example, sex (usually a beautiful woman), nationalism (a flag waving), or popular music. None of these is a good reason for buying something like a car.

Example: Fly with the Eagle from Patriot Motors—like you, proud to be American.

9. *Consumer Fill-In:* This is a highly specialized technique. A company will construct an advertisement in which it leaves something out that people normally expect to hear; thus, people are led to add that missing part, which makes the product or service seem more than it really is. The missing part is often the word "only" or the superlative "the most."

Example: Among the leading razors, (only?) Blade Runner gives men on the go a double-edged shave.

Of all the chairs you can sit in, you'll find Fundament the (most?) *satisfying* one.

10. *Word Play and Slogans:* Play with language catches a person's attention and interest—the first step in persuading him or her to buy. Using a common saying or idiom in a different context and sometimes changing the saying slightly are frequently used techniques. All of the above examples except the "like" sentence in number 1 include word play that would serve the advertiser well, and the "like" example has its own kind of word play, a simile. Using slogans (short attention-getting expressions) is also a popular technique, especially as they are repeated and made part of an extended advertising campaign. The word play below could also be a slogan with a long life span.

Example: Springer Basketball Shoes: We get the jump.

Now evaluate the ten advertising statements that you will hear on the tape. Decide which techniques they use. You may find more than one technique in a statement—that is, a main technique plus one or two others. Include information from the statements to support your evaluations.

1. _____
_____

2. _____
_____

3. _____
_____

4. _____
_____

5. _____
_____

6. _____
_____

7. _____
_____

8. _____
_____

9. _____
_____

10. _____
_____

Exercise 5—Student Advertising Statements

Create your own advertising statements based on the techniques described above. Share them in class. How well are the other students able to evaluate your statements, and how well are you able to evaluate theirs?

1. _____

2. _____

3. _____

4. _____

5. _____

6. _____

7. _____

8. _____

9. _____

10. _____

Exercise 6—Professional Advertising Statements

Bring to class at least three examples of advertisements that you find in print, or that you observe on television or radio and that you carefully note. On the lines below, evaluate these advertisements, referring to the above techniques as appropriate. Do you find any new techniques that you can categorize?

1. _____

2. _____

3. _____

Exercise 7—Evaluating Public Statements

On the lines below, copy or paraphrase accurately three recent public statements made by prominent public figures, especially political figures. The statements should be the kind that seek to influence public opinion—that try to persuade us about what we should believe or what actions we should support or take. Share these statements and evaluate them in class. Do they appear true, right, complete, balanced, fair, and so on? What criteria are the statements based on? Do you agree or disagree with the statements, in whole or in part? What are the criteria for your evaluation?

1. _____
   _____
   _____

2. _____
   _____
   _____

3. _____
   _____
   _____

Exercise 8—Discussion: Self in Relation to Others

The central issue in *The Case of Life or Death* and in the follow-up evaluating that you did, especially with regard to ethical questions, was the consideration of self in relation to others. How much emphasis should an individual place on himself or herself? How much emphasis should a group or nation place on itself? Read the following discussion questions, which are connected with this subject, and choose one or more to talk about. Before you begin discussing them, however, study the information on the next page about leader and nonparticipant roles in discussions so that you will be able to understand and function well as a discussion participant.

Discussion Questions

1. Is pride—individual, national, ethnic, or racial—a good thing? At what point does it stop being good?

2. Ambitiousness is sometimes seen as a good thing and sometimes as a bad thing. Where does it stop being good and become bad?

3. How important is competition for human development? Where should competition end and cooperation begin?

4. How much individualism is good? When does it become selfishness?

5. What is the responsibility of a successful individual or nation to those that are less successful, especially those that have helped provide for the individual's or nation's success?

6. What basic responsibilities do people and nations have toward one another?

7. How much trust can an individual or a nation have in others? How does one judge the right amount of trust? Why is trust important?

Leader and Nonparticipant Roles in Discussions

As the discussion section in chapter 13 pointed out, understanding the roles that you can play in group discussions can help you improve your participation in them. It can also help you improve your overall ability to listen, think, and speak in English. The discussion section in chapter 13 described the general "participant orientations." The information below is about the roles of leader and nonparticipant.

The role of leader can be assigned, or it can develop naturally within a group. There are four types that may be considered.

1. *Controlling Leader.* This kind of leader generally controls, directs, or acts as the authority in a discussion. The controlling leader assumes this role by appointment, by individual preference, or by necessary choice because others are less involved.

2. *Guiding Leader.* This kind of leader sets direction for or helps to guide a discussion instead of controlling it. The guiding leader is open to and desirous of others' participation; he or she will allow or even welcome a sharing of leadership.

3. *Relaxed Leader.* This kind of leader sets a minimum of direction for a discussion, preferring to let it go naturally wherever it may. He or she is usually a leader who has been appointed.

4. *Nonleader.* This kind of leader sets no direction at all for a discussion. He or she may be a leader who was appointed but who does not lead. Nonleaders may also be individuals who work together equally well or equally poorly (a successful sharing of discussion without one clear leader most likely involves several people taking turns guiding or setting direction).

For the role of nonparticipant, there are also four types that may be considered.

1. *Silent but Attentive Nonparticipant* ("tuned in"): This kind of nonparticipant does not talk at any length, but he or she follows the discussion and may show involvement through body language and some brief verbal responses.

2. *Silent and Inattentive Nonparticipant* ("tuned out"): This kind of nonparticipant does not talk and does not care about the discussion.

3. *Digressive Nonparticipant:* This kind of nonparticipant talks (possibly jokes) about things other than the subject under discussion.

4. *Negative Nonparticipant:* This kind of nonparticipant says negative, unconstructive things or just complains about the subject or task under discussion.

As with the participant orientations, all of the above are natural ways to be, and generally a person does not function in any one way exclusively. What is important is (1) gaining awareness of what you do in a discussion and (2) trying different roles to benefit the discussion and yourself.

Apply all of the knowledge you have gained about roles—participant, leader, and nonparticipant—to the discussion activity above. After the discussion, you and your classmates may gain in awareness by sharing perceptions about one another's performance.

16 The Case of Life or LIFE

Prelistening: The Situation

Before Sherlock Holmes XIII has had a chance to unravel the thoughts and feelings of the Oge Retla and decide whether or not to open the north pole vault in *The Case of Life or Death*, a second message is found. This message is in the form of a tape, made by the last of the Oge Retla leaders just before his death. This final piece of information will be crucial in the life or death decision that Holmes XIII has to make. Actually, as the tape soon makes clear, the decision will be even more fundamental than life or death—it will be a matter of life or LIFE!

Instructions

1. There are ten sections in the taped account of this case. There will be time after each section for you to evaluate the Oge Retla's desire—to judge whether they want the Earth people to live or to die. Write your evaluations and your reasons for them as simply and as quickly as you can on the numbered lines below.

2. Listen carefully and think carefully about your basis for judging. Are the criteria for evaluating mostly external to you? Do they become more internal in later sections? After listening to and evaluating all ten sections, make a final evaluation of the complete message.

Evaluations and Reasons for Them

1. _____
2. _____
3. _____
4. _____
5. _____
6. _____
7. _____
8. _____
9. _____
10. _____

Final Evaluation and Reasons for It

What is your judgment of the Oge Retla's final desire?

_____
_____

Questions

Answer these questions orally or in writing.

1. How much do the Oge Retla blame the Earth people for what has happened to them?

2. To what earlier situation on Earth does the speaker compare the situation on Htrae? What is the point of the comparison?

3. Why does the speaker say that for the Oge Retla to kill the Earth people would be like killing themselves?

4. The speaker also says that the Earth people are already dying: In what way are they dying?

5. What does the speaker foresee the Earth people doing in the future if they continue to live in the same way?

6. Does the speaker see any hope for the Earth people? Explain.

7. What does the speaker suggest about the vault containing nuclear fuel?

8. After listening to this message, what do you think is in the north-pole vault? Why do you think so?

9. Based on the entire taped message, what do you think the speaker wants the Earth people to do? Why doesn't the speaker simply tell the Earth people what to do?

10. If you were Holmes XIII and the Earth people, what would you do in this situation? Why?

11. What is the significance of the title of this case?

Listening Skill: Evaluating— Clarifying Values

Becoming more active in listening, evaluating, and speaking—in *evaluative listening and speaking*—can improve your second language ability significantly. In fact, becoming more aware of how you evaluate and of the criteria that you use— in the context of a different language and culture and in relation to people of different backgrounds—can greatly enrich your overall linguistic, cognitive, and affective functioning. The exercises in this chapter will give you more practice in *clarifying your values* in English in this way.

Exercise 1—Clarifying Values: A New Civilization

Imagine that the planet Earth is being invaded by aliens from outer space. The people on earth will not be able to survive this invasion. A spaceship has been prepared to help a hastily selected number of people escape in order to begin a new civilization elsewhere in the universe. Unfortunately, the original selection of eleven people is too large. There is now room for only seven people.

Your task is to choose the four people who will have to stay behind on Earth and therefore die. Put the number 1 next to the first person you believe should stay. Then put the number 2 next to the second person, the number 3 next to the third person, and the number 4 next to the fourth person.

The class will then be divided into small groups. Each group must decide on the same four people and in the same order (the same order is necessary in the event of any last-minute changes). You will have only twenty minutes to do this before the spaceship leaves. Use all of the time to think, discuss, and decide. Listen to one another and evaluate carefully. What are you looking for in the seven people who will attempt to begin a new civilization? What will be most important, of most value? After your group finishes, compare your results with the other groups' results.

___ A ballerina

___ A truck driver

___ The truck driver's pregnant wife

___ A young farm boy

___ A retired religious leader

___ An army officer with a gun

___ A dentist

___ An under-graduate student in astrophysics

___ A successful playwright

___ An Olympic heavyweight boxing champion

___ A girl with high honors in junior high school

Note: After you finish the discussion activity, your teacher may ask you to review the discussion roles that people played in their groups.

Exercise 2—Clarifying Values: UFO Crash

Imagine that you and the other members of your group (determined by your teacher) are out in the country, far from any means of communication. A UFO crash-lands very close to where you are. A series of increasingly stronger explosions in one part of the UFO begin to rock the spacecraft and suggest that it will all explode within a short time, perhaps thirty minutes.

Your group must decide what to do. If you *all* work together, there is a possibility that you can get into the spacecraft and rescue any survivors or any valuable information that is inside. You would risk death and possibly other dangers. If you choose not to do this as a group, the spacecraft and all it contains will be lost. You have a maximum of fifteen minutes to decide what your group will do. Use the time to think, discuss, and decide. Do not be hasty—have carefully thought out reasons for your group's decision.

As in the first exercise, listen to one another and evaluate carefully. What values do you have to clarify in order to make a decision? What criteria will be the basis for your decision? After your group and the other groups finish making a decision, compare your decision-making processes as well as your results.

Note: After you finish the discussion activity, your teacher may ask you to review the discussion roles that people played in their groups.

Exercise 3—Interview about Values

You and a classmate will interview each other about the five things in life that are most important to each of you. These will be the things that you believe are necessary in order to have a good life. Complete your individual list of values before asking your classmate about his or her list. Discuss the reasons for the choices that each of you makes. Also discuss the things that each of you does in order to achieve or maintain the things that are listed.

Your list of values:	Your classmate's list:
1. _____	1. _____
2. _____	2. _____
3. _____	3. _____
4. _____	4. _____
5. _____	5. _____

After you finish interviewing each other, share your findings with the rest of the class. What values do you hold in common? What perceptions, insights, or understandings do you gain that might help you in considering or reconsidering your own values?

Exercise 4—Free Association

Sometimes the way we think and talk about values is different, without our knowing it, from the way we feel about them deep inside ourselves. The result is that we may really act or live, in accordance with our deeply felt values, in a way that is different from how we think and talk. Because of this, tension may result. It can be helpful to try to get at our inner values in order to understand them and to deal with them in a way that will reduce conflict between thought and action.

An exercise that can tell more about inner values is "free association." You will hear a list of words and phrases on the tape. After you hear each word or phrase, immediately write the first association (related word or idea) that comes to your mind. You will not have time to stop and think. The free associations you give will most likely tell you something about your inner values.

1. _____ 16. _____

2. _____ 17. _____

3. _____ 18. _____

4. _____ 19. _____

5. _____ 20. _____

6. _____ 21. _____

7. _____ 22. _____

8. _____ 23. _____

9. _____ 24. _____

10. _____ 25. _____

11. _____ 26. _____

12. _____ 27. _____

13. _____ 28. _____

14. _____ 29. _____

15. _____ 30. _____

Exercise 5—Matching Qualities

Use the list of adjectives, below, that describe human qualities to make two separate ten-word lists of your own. One list will be the qualities that you value most in yourself. The other list will be the qualities that you value most in a friend.

After everyone in class has finished writing, walk around and talk about yourselves and the kinds of friends you prefer (refer to your lists to help you remember). If two students have ten or more qualities on their lists that match, they may be considered to have an overall match.

Your Most Valued Qualities	Most Valued Qualities in a Friend
1. _____	1. _____
2. _____	2. _____
3. _____	3. _____
4. _____	4. _____
5. _____	5. _____
6. _____	6. _____
7. _____	7. _____
8. _____	8. _____
9. _____	9. _____
10. _____	10. _____

kind	artistic
friendly	scientific
funny	generous
serious	outgoing
quiet	curious
talkative	adventurous
relaxed	modest
energetic	respectful
even-tempered	selfless
well-mannered	competitive
caring	cooperative
forgiving	religious
loyal	humanistic
ambitious	fair-minded
helpful	easygoing
good-looking	creative
intelligent	analytical
sweet	gentle
independent	hard-working
musical	conscientious
honest	firm
patient	flexible
nonsexist	modern
gracious	traditional
warm	considerate
practical	open-minded
imaginative	accepting
intellectual	understanding
spontaneous	thoughtful
deliberate	active

Are there any qualities listed above that you do not possess that you would like to develop? Are there any qualities that you would like to add to the general list? These are matters that you may wish to make part of class discussion.

Exercise 6—Evaluating Qualities

Listen to the five statements about Barbara that use words from the list above and that add details related to those qualities. After each statement, write on the numbered lines below whether the statement is mainly *approving* or *disapproving*. Also add a key word or two from the statement to support your evaluation.

1. _____
   Key words: _____
   _____

2. _____
   Key words: _____
   _____

3. _____
   Key words: _____
   _____

4. _____
   Key words: _____
   _____

5. _____
   Key words: _____
   _____

Overall, are the statements approving or disapproving? _____

Exercise 7—Student Statements about Qualities

Create a fictitious person and write five statements about the person's qualities. Draw from the qualities listed above, add some details, and try to capture the complexity of the person's character. You may want to think about qualities that you have seen in real people to help you write your statements. The rest of the class will listen to your statements and decide if they are *approving* or *disapproving*, first one at a time and then overall. Also, you will evaluate the other students' statements about their fictitious persons.

Plan your five statements here.

1. _____
   _____
   _____

2. _____
   _____
   _____

3. _____
   _____
   _____

4. _____
   _____
   _____

5. _____
   _____
   _____

Exercise 8—Discussion: Development

The crucial issue in *The Case of Life or LIFE* was development—of people and of nations. Read the following discussion questions, about development, and choose one or more to talk about. First, though, test your memory of the different leader and nonparticipant roles that may be played in a discussion. List them in the review section on the next page. Review these roles and the "participant orientations" in order to help yourself understand and function well in the discussion activity.

Discussion Questions

1. Do you agree that human development in general has been much stronger intellectually than emotionally? Explain.

2. If your answer to the first question is affirmative, what problems do you think have resulted or may result in the future?

3. Do you agree with the perception that the Earth is being expended or wasted away? Explain.

4. Are you in favor of the development and use of nuclear energy (a focus in the two-part Oge Retla story), or not? Explain your reasons.

5. What nonnuclear sources of energy, if any, would you like to see developed and used? In general, what energy policies would you like to see? Explain your reasons.

6. What scientific and technological advances have been made that improve the quality of LIFE? Which ones have had the opposite effect?

7. How can we make advances in the physical world and still preserve and protect the quality of LIFE in all respects? Are there any general proposals that you might make?

8. What general plan could you recommend to help people develop their various kinds of potential, including the potential for being more humane? What kinds of education and experience would you recommend?

9. What general plan could you recommend to help nations develop their own kinds of potential, once again including the potential for being more humane? What national and international policies would you recommend?

Review: Leader and Nonparticipant Roles in Discussions

How many types of leaders and types of nonparticipants can you remember. Only after you have checked your memory completely should you refer to the information at the end of chapter 15.

Leader Types	Nonparticipant Types
1. _____	1. _____
2. _____	2. _____
3. _____	3. _____
4. _____	4. _____

After you complete the discussion activity, review all the discussion roles that people played.

Exercise 9—Presentations: Personal Development

Make a five-to-seven-minute presentation about how you have developed during the current term of study or during a longer period of time (for example, one, two, five, or ten years). Focus on information that will be interesting and possibly helpful to your audience.

Another option is to present information about how you plan to develop over a particular period of time in the future. Again, focus on matters that will be interesting and potentially instructive.

Remember to (1) carefully plan and organize your presentation, (2) use specific language, (3) offer visual aids if appropriate and helpful, (4) support your speaking with body language, (5) use an appropriate attention-getter, and (6) use your voice as an instrument to aid communication. Also, study the information below about closings; it will further help you to prepare for your presentation.

Closings in Presentations

Many people believe that the ending is the second most important part of a presentation. It is what you will leave your audience with. It therefore should not be anything weak like, "Well, that's all," "I guess that's all," "That's it," or "I don't have anything else to say." At the same time, you should neither drag to a close nor end abruptly. There is a need to round off, to give a sense of completeness, and to create the right final effect—a strong effect if possible. Here are some common ways to close a presentation.

1. Summarize your main points, in a fresh and forceful way if possible. This is especially useful in longer presentations.

2. Save your strongest point for the end, to use as a kind of climax. This may be a conclusion after adding up or considering different points.

3. As with number 2, save a strong detail that is appropriate for the end, possibly something unexpected, surprising, or even funny. This could be a quotation or possibly a short anecdote.

4. Call the audience to action. Even if you are talking mainly about yourself, if you can involve the members of the audience in thinking about what they should do too, then it can be a strong ending. You may want to use a question for this purpose.

5. Look toward the future or toward some kind of extension of your presentation. Your talk may be the kind that allows for a brief consideration of what may follow, develop, or result in the future. You may want to use a question for this purpose, too.

Develop an effective closing from one of these possibilities to suit your presentation, above. In general, focus on ending all of the presentations that you give as completely and as strongly as possible.

Roles and Clues

1. The telephone company reports that 293-9690 is not a working number.

2. Main Motive Clue (five parts): (1) a payment for parking or driving a car against the law: a _____.

3. The private secretary: You last saw Pennypacker at 5:00 P.M., closing time, and he told you that he was going to get the astrophysicist a role in the next *Star Wars* movie.

4. The message contains three words.

5. The telephone number should be counted on to solve the mystery.

6. Freddie Rockbottom, son of John D. Rockbottom: playing video games—since breakfast—hundreds of games.

7. Professor Grapesun was disappointed when he was not selected as the new president of the university.

8. The custodian: You saw Pennypacker at about 4:30 P.M., and he told you that he was going to give the head typist a new space-age dicta-typewriter.

9. Sentences come before words in this case—three of each.

10. King Tut's wife had a very small wrist.

11. President Hardacre began to have trouble with his office air conditioner about two weeks ago.

12. The butler: polishing silverware—since 1:30—about 36 pieces.

13. Pettibone was a criminal all his life, and he even obstructed justice in his death.

14. 9 follows 2, 3, and 6.

15. The financial officer: You saw Pennypacker at 2:30 P.M., and he told you that he was going to give the spaceship pilot a 25 percent raise in salary.

16. Main Motive Clue (five parts): (3) a turtle's back: a _____.

17. GD wants Emma to "dial his letter" in order to find the hidden earrings.

18. The mathematical difference between the first pair of letters is eight—between the second pair, eight again—between the third pair . . .

19. Ms. Peartree was not happy about having to work overtime on the university's financial situation, especially after President Hardacre prevented her from getting a new job as a research assistant in the university's anthropology department.

20. The housing director: You talked to Pennypacker by telephone at 9:30 A.M., and he told you that he was going to build a new research laboratory for the head of the medical team.

21. Dr. Watson: Follow the example questioning on page 14. Ask the same underlined questions for each suspect and repeat the information that you hear.

22. Odd before even.

23. One might say that 293-9690 has a jarring telephone ring.

24. The laundress: washing and drying clothes in the basement—for 5 hours— 5 loads of clothes.

25. Method Clue (three parts): (3) a place to sit: a _____.

26. The vice president: You saw Pennypacker in a meeting at 3:00 P.M.; he told you that there was one person that he had to fire because of "work problems," but he did not name the person.

27. Code Clue: S = S.

28. 293-9690 is not a wrong number.

29. Mrs. Snowden disliked President Hardacre's jokes and complaints about the cafeteria food.

30. The Chauffeur: washing and waxing cars—since lunch—6 cars.

31. B through T comes before the first I through the last E.

32. The geologist: You saw Pennypacker on his way to lunch at 12:00 P.M., and he told you that he was going to give the mining engineer a state-of-the-art computer with artificial intelligence.

33. The handyman: painting rooms in the guest house—since 8:30—6 rooms.

34. Drummond had prearranged with Emma Raleigh to communicate with her through the Miss Lonelyhearts section of the newspaper.

35. Code Clue: E = E.

36. Perpetrator Clue: a type of weather: _____.

37. The accountant: You saw Pennypacker during a break at 10:15 A.M., and he told you that he was going to give the social director her own personal Space Invaders video game.

38. The cook: peeling potatoes and chopping carrots—for 2 hours—about 50 potatoes and 40 carrots.

39. Mr. Rainberry felt that the maintenance budget had been unfairly reduced.

40. The earrings are in Drummond's apartment—somewhere.

41. Code Clue: B = B.

42. Felicia Rockbottom, daughter of John D. Rockbottom: playing songs on the piano—for a couple of hours—20 to 30 songs.

43. Assistant to Inspector Lestrade: Ask the suspects who they are, when they last saw or talked to Pennypacker, and what he talked to them about.

44. When Drummond's partners in crime and the police searched his apartment for the earrings, they looked in every conceivable place—almost.

45. Main Motive Clue (five parts): (5) a third person singular subject pronoun: _____.

46. Divide oddly and evenly and you will get the whole.

47. The downstairs maid: vacuuming rugs—for 2½ hours—13 rugs.

48. The head typist: You talked to Pennypacker around 11:15 P.M., and he told you that he was going to give the custodian an automatic floor sweeper and window washer.

49. GD's letter to Miss Lonelyhearts attempts to take the lid off the earrings' hiding place.

50. Code Clue: N = N.

51. Mrs. Snowden, Ms. Peartree, Mr. Rainberry, and Professor Grapesun often ate lunch together and met socially.

52. Drummond jammed the earrings into a place where no one would think to look for them.

53. Inspector Lestrade: Follow the example questioning on page 14. Ask the same underlined questions for each suspect and repeat the information that you hear.

54. The managing director: You saw Pennypacker after lunch, around 1:30 P.M., and he told you that he was going to buy a robot messenger for the mining operation foreman.

55. Main Motive Clue (five parts): (4) a past form of the verb be: _____.

56. Code Clue: I = I.

57. The astrophysicist: You saw Pennypacker briefly at 9:00 A.M., and he told you that he had finally decided to ask his private secretary to marry him.

58. Abigail Rockbottom, wife of John D. Rockbottom: writing letters—all day—14 letters.

59. A "hot seat" is a slang term for (1) a difficult position to be in or (2) a method of executing persons who have been sentenced to death.

60. The digits in the telephone number have a special meaning.

61. Code Clue: L = L.

62. The social director: You talked to Pennypacker by telephone around 2:00 P.M., and he told you that he had bought a gold bar paperweight for the accountant.

63. Besides working as a secretary, Ms. Peartree was a part-time anthropology student who specialized in studying primitive religious beliefs in the West Indies.

64. R follows B, as C follows A, as . . .

65. The Secretary to Mr. Rockbottom: paying bills—since noon—about 22 bills.

66. 2 is to 9, as 3 is to 9, as 6 is to 9, as 0 is to nothing.

67. Method Clue (three parts): (2) a magician closes his show with his biggest ———.

68. The mining engineer: You saw Pennypacker coming back from lunch at 1:00 P.M., and he told you that he was going to give the geologist some precious rock samples from the planet Venus.

69. Code Clue: D = D.

70. Professor Grapesun's major research in electrical engineering was in remote-control devices.

71. Drummond knew how hot the earrings were (he knew how hotly they would be searched for), so he decided to cool them off.

72. Assistant to Inspector Lestrade: Follow the example questioning on page 14. Ask the same underlined questions for each suspect and repeat the information that you hear.

73. The lawyer: You saw Pennypacker in a private meeting at 5:30 P.M., and he told you that he was going to turn over control of the company to the vice president.

74. Code Clue: R = R.

75. Drummond knew he was in a sticky situation, so he acted accordingly.

76. The spaceship pilot: You saw Pennypacker over a cup of coffee around 10:30 A.M., and he told you that he was going to transfer one thousand shares of company stock to the financial officer.

77. Sherlock Holmes: Follow the example questioning on page 14. Ask the same underlined questions for each suspect and repeat the information that you hear.

78. Main Motive Clue (five parts): (2) an industrious insect that often appears at picnics: an ———.

79. Drummond wanted to preserve the earrings for Emma Raleigh and himself.

80. Code Clue: C = C.

81. The trainer for Mr. Rockbottom: doing push-ups, sit-ups, and other exercises—for about an hour and a half—200 push-ups, 200 sit-ups, and quite a few other exercises.

82. The head of the medical team: You talked to Pennypacker by telephone at about 10:00 A.M., and he told you that he was going to present the housing director with a vacation home on the moon.

83. Mr. Rainberry was an expert electrician.

84. Drummond believed somewhat literally in the idea of stolen jewelry as "ice."

85. First is first, but third is second, and so on.

86. The dishwasher: washing pots and pans—since about 1:00—23 pots and 19 pans.

87. Method Clue (three parts): (1) a word that means to vote a person into a political office: to ———.

88. Dr. Watson: Ask the suspects who they are, when they last saw or talked to Pennypacker, and what he talked to them about.

89. Code Clue: A = A.

90. Drummond used only butter on his toast on the day that he hid the earrings.

91. The gardener: planting flowers—for 3½ hours—2 flowers.

92. Perpetrator Clue: a fruit: ———.

93. Code Clue: M = M.

94. Sherlock Holmes: Ask the suspects who they are, when they last saw or talked to Pennypacker, and what he talked to them about.

95. Pettibone had a very fine taste for jewelry.

96. Drummond was a terrible punster—a joker or player with words—as you can see at the end of his letter to Miss Lonelyhearts. Many of the clues to the case imitate his punning behavior.

97. The valet to Mr. Rockbottom: ironing shirts—all afternoon—20 to 25 shirts.

98. Mrs. Snowden's major hobbies were doll making and photography.

99. Code Clue: T = T.

100. Inspector Lestrade: Ask the suspects who they are, when they last saw or talked to Pennypacker, and what he talked to them about.

101. Drummond was sweet on his Emma—but also on jewelry.

102. The groundskeeper: washing the outside windows—since 10:00—60 to 70 windows.

103. President Hardacre always sat at his desk when he did any work in his office.

104. The mining operation foreman: You last saw Pennypacker at lunch, and he told you he was going to promote the managing director to vice president.

105. Holmes does not find the solution to this mystery to be especially difficult since he soon exclaims, "It's alimentary, my dear fellow!"

106. As usual, Sherlock Holmes's careful analysis and synthesis of information proved to be fruitful in solving this case.

Scripts

*CHAPTER 1
The Case of the Treasure Hunt, or "The Secret to Success"
Directions
First, enter Contemplation Common from the northwest corner.

Then, go straight to the Fountain of Life.

Next, walk around the north side of the fountain.

After that, go to the corner of the Science Building next to the rose garden.

Then, walk back around the east side of the fountain and continue on to the newsstand.

Now go back and complete your circle of the fountain.

Stop so that you face the statue of Socrates.

Finally, go to the information stand in the southeast corner.

That is all. *X* marks the spot of the treasure—and *O* marks the spot also! There you will find "The Secret of Success."

Exercise 4
Directions
First, draw a horizontal line.

Second, from the horizontal line's right endpoint, draw upward a vertical line one-half as long.

Third, from the midpoint of the horizontal line, draw downward and to the left a diagonal line the same length as the vertical line.

Last, connect the endpoints of the diagonal line with a semicricle on the bottom side, facing up.

*CHAPTER 2
Exercise 3
Directions (to be given by the teacher in class)
1. The Rockbottom mansion is in the center of the picture.

2. A road runs horizontally along the bottom of the picture.

3. A semicircular driveway runs from the road up to the front of the mansion and back down to the road.

4. Before the driveway reaches the mansion, a smaller driveway branches on the right to a garage below and to the right of the mansion.

5. In the center of the lawn inside the main driveway, there is a large apple tree.

6. There is a row of rose bushes leading from the garage to the mansion.

7. There is a row of flowers leading from the left side of the mansion, along the driveway, to a small guest house.

8. Directly behind the mansion there is a complete flower garden.

9. Diagonally behind the mansion and the guest house, there is a round swimming pool.

10. Diagonally behind the mansion and the garage, there is a tennis court.

11. There are three small hills in the upper left hand corner of the picture.

12. A path leads from the right side of the mansion, between the flower garden and the tennis court, to a sailboat on the ocean in the upper-right-hand corner.

Exercise 5
Joke Number One
A. Why did the chicken cross the road?
B. I don't know—why did the chicken cross the road?
A. To get to the other side!

Joke Number Two
A. Why did the chicken cross the road?
B. I don't know—why?
A. For some fowl reason.

Joke Number Three
A. I had to take my husband to the doctor because he thought he was a chicken.
B. Did the doctor help?
A. No, he didn't.
B. That's too bad.
A. Well, not completely. At least we don't have to buy eggs anymore.

*CHAPTER 3
The Case of the Missing Bracelet
Lestrade: It's the end of a bad business, Mr. Holmes. It's over with. Convict Henry Pettibone died this morning in his sleep in the infirmary of Dartmoor Prison. The cause of death has not been determined, but we suspect cancer or some other disease of the intestinal area.

Holmes: Hmm, Henry Pettibone . . . Inspector Lestrade, isn't Pettibone the thief who stole the famous Tut gold bracelet, the one that King Tutankhamen of Egypt gave to his wife over 3000 years ago?

Lestrade: Yes, of course, Pettibone's the one. And the bracelet's the one that was found by Sir Ralph Teasdale during a scientific study at one of the pyramids in Egypt. Sir Ralph gave the bracelet to his wife, Lady Diana Teasdale.

Holmes: And of course it was Pettibone who stole the bracelet from Lady Teasdale while she was staying at the Copley Hotel.

Lestrade: But it didn't do him any good, if you remember, Mr. Holmes. We arrested him shortly afterward as he was trying to make his escape from the hotel.

Holmes: Unfortunately, though, the bracelet disappeared after it was stolen. Pettibone didn't have it on him when you arrested him. But I don't understand why Pettibone didn't try to communicate with someone about the bracelet if he knew he was dying.

Lestrade: But he did, Mr. Holmes. That's why I've come to see you. After three years in prison, he finally wrote this note to his mother, but he was unable to mail it before he died. It's in a secret code, and we can't figure it out.

Holmes: I don't have my glasses. Please read it to me.

Lestrade: It goes like this: BIRNASCIEDLEEMTE.

Holmes: All right, let me make sure that I wrote that down correctly. That's BIRNASCIEDLEEMTE. Very good, now let's have a crack at it!

Exercise 1
Situations
1. Teacher: Good morning, everyone. We'll move on to some new material later on in class. First, though, I'd like to begin by reviewing the work we were doing last time on page 112 of your textbook.

2. Bus driver: Well, the traffic is a little heavy for this time of day, but now that we've made our way around the corner, if you'll look out to the right you'll catch a glimpse of the Washington Monument.

3. Consumer: Let's see, well, if I have to replace this old beat-up pocket watch of mine, I might as well really get into the swing of things and try something flashy for a change—how about letting me see that wristwatch with the rainbow face up on the top shelf?

4. Airline employee: Well, that takes care of everything. You're all ready to board your flight. All you have to do is go through gate 27.

5. Supermarket employee: I'm pretty sure the store carries the kind of rice you're looking for. Check over in aisle 9A first, and if you can't find it there, then you might try aisle 3B.

Exercise 2
Conversation Number One
A man is at the airport. He asks a car rental attendant for some directions.

A. Excuse me. Could you tell me how to get to the Trade Center?

B. Sure, that's easy. Go up Broadway until you reach Main Street. The Hart Hotel will be on the right. Turn right onto Main Street and then take your second left. Go about a block and you'll see the Trade Center on the right.

Where is the Trade Center? Write your answer.

Conversation Number Two
A woman has just come out of the Hart Hotel. She asks the hotel doorman for some directions.

A. Excuse me. Could you tell me the way to the Strand movie theater?

B. Yes, I can. Head straight up north here to Fremont and turn right. Then take your first left, in the direction of the shopping mall. You'll pass through two intersections, and then you'll want to turn left at the third one. Go one more block and you'll find the theater.

Where is the movie theater? Write your answer.

Conversation Number Three
A couple has just come out of the concert hall. The man asks a policeman for some help.

A. Good evening, officer. Could you tell us how to get to the Stardust Cafe?

B. No problem. Go west on Fremont past Broadway. You'll want the second right after that and then your second left. You'll take one more right, the next one you see, and at the next intersection you'll find the cafe.

Where is the cafe? Write your answer.

Conversation Number Four
A woman is leaving the shopping mall. She asks another shopper for some directions.

A. I wonder if you could possibly tell me how to get to the new French bakery?

B. That's not too hard. Let's see ... drive over to Pulaski and go on down past Main Street in the direction of the high school. Turn left to go to the high school, but take your first right before you get to it. Halfway down that road you'll find the bakery.

Where is the bakery? Write your answer.

Conversation Number Five
A group of visiting international students is at the high school. They ask the principal for some directions to their next place to visit in Waterbury.

A. Our next stop is CCC, Contron Computer Corporation. Could you tell us how to get there?

B. Yes, I can. Let's see—drive up to Main Street and take a left. Go past Pulaski and then take your second left. Keep on going until you come to a fork in the road. Bear left at the fork, and keep on that until you see another road entering from the right. That's where you'll find Contron—at that intersection.

Where is Contron Computer Corporation? Write your answer.

Exercise 5
News Report
At a news conference today in Washington, Secretary of State Henry Greenspan announced his plans for an important diplomatic world tour. For details, we turn to our Washington correspondent, Roger Muller.

Secretary of State Henry Greenspan's announcement today that he plans to visit leading officials in six different countries next April suggests the development of a new and more active American foreign policy.

Mr. Greenspan will leave Washington and arrive in Paris on April 14 for a series of meetings with foreign ministers from Western Europe. The major topic of discussion will be plans for new negotiations with the Soviet Union regarding nuclear arms control, especially in Europe.

Following that, Mr. Greenspan will arrive in Khartoum, Sudan on April 17. There he will join representatives from several African nations in reviewing ways to help fight present and future food shortages.

On April 20, Mr. Greenspan's itinerary takes him to Riyadh, Saudi Arabia. His efforts there will be to demonstrate the United States' desire for improved relations with all nations in the Middle East and for peace throughout the region.

Beijing is the next stop on the diplomatic tour. The meetings scheduled to begin on April 22 will focus on China's new open-door policy for foreign investment and technological development.

Moving on to Tokyo on the twenty-fourth, Mr. Greenspan will examine trade relations with Japanese officials. He will also review Japan's efforts to ensure its own national security.

Finally, before returning to Washington on the twenty-eighth, the Secretary will visit Mexico City on the twenty-sixth and twenty-seventh. He will discuss with representatives from several Latin American countries two areas of major concern: the economic policies that the United States and the other nations are following and the current political situation throughout Central America.

Mr. Greenspan has a lot of diplomatic homework to do before he begins his tour, and he will surely have a lot when he returns. But both here in Washington and abroad, people are looking for good results from all of the hard work to come. This is Roger Muller, in Washington.

Exercise 6
Movie Critiques
Good evening and welcome to Peek Previews at the Movies, the program that informs you about the new movies that are coming to the theaters. Five new major films are opening across the U.S. this week, and there is definitely an international flavor to them.

We will begin with a surprising comedy from Japan, *Zatoichi vs. Godzilla*. The entertaining thing about this movie is the way it combines two kinds of movies that are very different—the samurai movie and the monster movie. The result is a wildly funny comedy. There is so much action in it and I laughed so hard that it was difficult for me to read all the subtitles. One small problem is that we know from the beginning who will win the fight between the two title characters. The only suspense is in *how* he will win.

Our second new arrival is the French biographical film, *de Gaulle*, starring Yves Montand as the famous French general and leader. The strength of the movie is its careful recording of historical facts. The major problem is in the portrayal of de Gaulle. It is always difficult to act the part of a great and unique historical figure, but it is perhaps especially difficult with de Gaulle. Mr. Montand has been a great actor for many years, but de Gaulle's physical and personal characteristics are too difficult to capture. The film also may have only limited interest for audiences outside of France.

Next is the romantic adventure story *Around the World in Eighty Minutes*, from Mexico. This is a sequel to the great, classic 1950s movie *Around the World in Eighty Days*. Unlike most sequels, which usually fail to be as good as the original movies, this one is as good and perhaps even better for two reasons. First, its use of science fiction gives an old story new life in our advanced world of today. Second, the reappearance of the comic actor Cantinflas, this time in the romantic leading role, is a great delight. On a negative note, Cantinflas's rapid appearance and disappearance in so many different countries around the world results in a too brief and sometimes confusing view of their cultures.

From Italy comes the wild social satire *8½—13½—Hike!*, starring Laura Antonelli. Ms. Antonelli plays the coach of the Italian National Football Team, which challenges the American Super Bowl champion to a world championship game. Italian football, of course, is what Americans call soccer, which is very different from American football. At halftime the Italian team is losing by a score of 63 to 0, and it is only the appearance of the beautiful Ms. Antonelli in the American team's locker room that causes the Americans to forget the rest of the game and thus forfeit it to the Italians. Ms. Antonelli is wonderful in her role, but the story is too difficult to believe, even for a wild social satire.

Last is the one new American film opening this week, and it also is a kind of sequel. It brings together for the third time the actors Paul Newman and Robert Redford, although this time they are competing against each other as cowboy gangsters. This new modern tragedy is called *The Stung*. Actually, Newman and Redford both succeed as criminals, but fail as lovers. In a very moving scene, the woman they both love, Jane Fonda, throws them out of her exercise studio. The movie itself succeeds in showing the problems that some Americans have in caring too much about money and not enough about other people. One complaint that I have is that there is too much violence in the film. Also, we do not see enough of Ms. Fonda, who is a fine actress.

That's all for this week. Tune in again next week when Peek Previews at the Movies takes a look at the new teenage cinema.

*CHAPTER 4
The Case of "Why Is Today a Special Day?"
Speaker Number One
Something strange happened in the Smiths' house this afternoon. I'm their next-door neighbor on Cornell Street, and at about two this afternoon I heard a lot of noise over there, like Mr. Smith was yelling or something. He's been home a lot and hasn't been able to find a job. That has put a strain on the whole family, including Mrs. Smith, who works part time, and the two children—Janet, who's in high school, and little Joseph, who's still in elementary school, I think. Anyway, I hope nothing bad has happened.

Speaker Number Two
I deliver newspapers in one of the northwest neighborhoods of Waterbury, and I really got to see something weird this afternoon. Well, first of all, the Smiths stopped getting the paper about a month ago, but I still go past their house on my route. Anyway, today, I saw a TV truck pull up to their house, followed by a police car. Mrs. Smith came out of the house—Mr. Smith was behind her—and then she fell down on her knees, holding up a small piece of paper between her hands and saying the number 2352 over and over again. She was crying, but she seemed pretty happy. I'm going to call Joey and ask him about it, or maybe his big sister Jan will know.

Speaker Number Three
I'm a salesman for the Bob Fisher Toyota-Ford Dealership, and this evening I sold not one, but two cars to the Smith family. They live over on Northwest Cornell, 2352 to be exact, and they had some bad luck when the steel mill in town closed down and Mr. Smith lost his job. Tonight, though, Mr. Smith bought a new Toyota Supra for his wife and a Ford Mustang for his teenage daughter, Janet. And I heard him promise to get a new bicycle for little Joe Junior. I guess their luck must have changed for the better—a lot better.

Exercise 4
News: Weather and Its Effects
From Florida's northern panhandle to Miami Beach, Arctic air is covering the state, with many cities registering the lowest temperatures on record. It's being called the freeze of the century. And the past two nights of subfreezing temperatures have severely affected Florida's agricultural industry. NPR's Jo Miglino reports:

With 75 percent of Florida's citrus crops still on the trees, state agriculture officials say it will be weeks before the damage done by the freeze can be assessed. But today inspectors visited groves to begin that task. There they found oranges that had frozen into solid balls of ice. This cold-damaged fruit can still be used for juice. But tomorrow it's expected the state's Citrus Commission will call for the temporary embargo of fresh-fruit shipments from the state to prevent poor quality fruit from being sold.

Citrus is not the only crop to be damaged by the freeze. Florida's winter vegetables were also severely affected. State agriculture officials called the pepper, squash, and cucumber crops total losses.

But after two nights of trying to save their harvests, Florida farmers will get little rest tonight. Another hard freeze is expected and another cold front is predicted to cover the state this weekend.

This is Jo Miglino, National Public Radio, reporting.

Exercise 5
News Feature: Interview Format
Could you please describe the work to us?

Well, it's definitely a seat from, from, uh, an outhouse, and this happened to be what is known as a three-holer, and it had three separate openings . . .

Three . . . toilet seats?

Yeah, well, they're openings in the . . . where you would sit down and go to the bathroom, I guess, if you want to say that.

But these are not just any toilet seats. They come from a nineteenth-century Long Island outhouse, and thirty years ago they were decorated by Willem de Kooning, the modern art master. Charles Vanderveer is one-third owner of the three-hole "throne," and he is certain the unsigned work is de Kooning's.

Two of the covers are missing. One has the original cover. And he painted this—it was painted by him—for a croquet party. And, Mrs. de Kooning verified the fact that he painted it. Now, he didn't paint this thing with the idea that it was going to be a major piece of art work. That's not what we're saying. But what—when you look at this, you can see that it's in his style of that period. And he's just that kind of a painter that, when he was so—his mind was so into all the style he was using in painting in those days— that this is what he used to decorate the inside of this building.

What color, uh, are these outhouse . . .

White . . .

. . . seats?

The seat itself is painted in white, and it's, it's a medium where you painted with white paint, and before it was dry, you went over it with another color. And, th-they're blacks and blues in it.

Would anybody passing it know that it was a de Kooning? Would, or maybe they'd think it was a Jackson Pollock? Or . . .

Well, there's evidence there that Jackson Pollock did it, too.

Oh yeah?!

Pollock's book, uh, about his life—or that they wrote about him—he mentions the fact that, uh, in the book, that he went there in 1954—this is when they

were there—and that the house was rented by Franz Kline, Willem de Kooning . . . De Kooning, uh, supposedly recognized or says that he remembers Jackson Pollock being there and throwing paint around. He doesn't, nobody remembers, de Kooning doesn't remember painting this.

Now, this thing went up for auction? Is that right?

I was commissioned to sell the contents of this house. I went in there, and there was this particular object, and I said, "Well, I could sell that, too." And then when I took it out, the owners told me that it, it had been painted by de Kooning. So, when I put it up for auction, I mentioned this, and nobody, they— people laughed at me.

Uh-huh!

When it came time to sell it, it didn't go for anything, so I bought it, for fifty dollars. And then, after it, the auction, was over, I went up to the owners, who were there, and said, "Look, I bought in that seat, that outhouse seat, and if I can get it authenticated, then you will be part of this whole thing." So, I did get it authenticated by giving away one-third of it, and then—ownership—and then I gave, I talked to the other people, and they got, they still maintained the other third.

And now this is an original, uh, work by a major American artist. And what—you're going to put it up for sale?

It's a very unusual thing, to begin with. It's not a painting on canvas, and so forth and so on. It was offered for sale at both Sotheby's and Christie's, and they wrote back letters to us, saying that they didn't think that this was the kind of thing that would . . .

Ha-ha-ha-ha! . . .

. . . be sold at public auction.

Ha-ha-ha-ha! . . .

I don't know that—how they get away with that statement, because you can sell anything at public auction. Now, the next thing is to, uh, get the art world involved in this thing, and have somebody say what, what they feel it is.

You might be able to pick up a little something for this.

It might be worth some money.

Uh-huh.

It's worth more than fifty dollars.

Fifty dollars, indeed. The last de Kooning sold for over two million. Charles Vanderveer is an auctioneer in Bridgehampton, Long Island.

Exercise 6
Commentary

Mel, the husband of "All Things Considered" commentator Kim Williams, retired seventeen years ago. Kim has survived, she says, because she has followed five important rules:

The first rule for living with a retired husband comes from Mrs. Casey Stengel. For better or for worse, she said, but not for lunch. I've always followed that ever since Mel retired. He retired early. He was in his fifties, I was in my forties.

So then came rule number two. One or the other has to leave home for all or part of the day. By pure coincidence, I was offered a part-time teaching job. "I can't fix lunch," I said. "I have to go, and if I'm not home by five, would you, could you . . . ?"

That was rule number three. Turn over the kitchen and don't look back. You know what Satchel Paige said, "If you look back, things will gain on you." Well, if you turn over the kitchen to a retired husband, things will gain on you anyway, but don't look back.

Rule four. Treat him like a stranger. I mean, politely. Both people, retired, need a space all their own, even if it's only a corner behind a screen. The other cannot enter and talk, talk, talk. You have to knock, make an appointment.

Rule five is don't be Siamese twins. You know how retired people sometimes start telling a story. One starts and the other says, "That's not the way it was." Well, if you're not always together, each can tell his or her version of a story, a big lie, if you like. Doesn't matter.

These rules are only a start. Mel and I have been married thirty-three years. We'll have to change more rules as we go on. You have to keep shifting, like a donkey cart going around curves on a mountain road.

This is Kim Williams in Missoula, Montana.

Exercise 7
Extended News Report

Now, a historical footnote. Last week the United States announced it was boycotting any further hearings before the International Court of Justice in a case involving Nicaragua. That American action parallels a United States boycott before another international court in a case involving Nicaragua nearly eighty years ago. NPR's Bill Buzenberg tells the story.

There's a temptation to say once upon a time. Actually, it was in 1907. Various wars were waging in Central America then, notably between Nicaragua and Guatemala. The United States and Mexico decided to intervene diplomatically to see if they could halt these conflicts. With Mexican backing, President

Theodore Roosevelt called a conference in Washington of the five Central American nations. They came and met and finally agreed to a series of conventions, including one setting up something quite popular at the time called the Central American Court of Justice. American progressives thought this was a splendid idea. The court would be an experiment, with Central America as the laboratory, to see how far international law could be pushed as a way to prevent wars. Cornell University historian Walter LaFeber writes about what happened to the court in his latest book, called *Inevitable Revolutions*.

The court was very successful in its early years. It, for example, mediated a war between Honduras and El Salvador. It stopped that war. The court acted very rapidly. The five Central American justices acted with great responsibility and great wisdom, I might say.

So the court was working well. It even had agents in the field to make sure its rulings were carried out. Billionaire Andrew Carnegie donated $100,000 to house the court in a magnificent new building in Costa Rica. But in 1912 the United States started getting more involved in Central America, and thus more involved with the court. It was then that U.S. Marines began their twenty-year occupation of Nicaragua. Historian LaFeber says a revolution broke out then against the government those Marines were propping up.

The revolutionaries in Nicaragua tried to take their case to the Central American Court of Justice. And the United States, of course, would have none of that. Uh, and the Central American Court simply couldn't act because the United States wouldn't let it act. Uh, the moral of that was pretty clear, and that is the Central American Court of Justice simply was not an operative court if the United States would not allow cases to be taken to it or the cases to be enforced.

The final blow to the court came four years later, in 1916. The United States had signed a treaty with the government it supported in Nicaragua, giving the United States rights to a canal and naval base in Nicaragua. The other Central American countries strongly objected since some of their rights were being given away, too. They took their case to the Central American Court, and the court once again ruled in their favor against the United States.

President Woodrow Wilson at that time simply said that they weren't, that we were not going to abide by the court's decision. We didn't care what the court said. We were going to build that naval base if we wanted and build the canal if we wanted in Nicaragua. That was the end of the Central American Court of Justice.

LaFeber says traditionally Central Americans have wanted to work closely with international courts, the League of Nations, and later the United Nations. He explains why:

It has been through these organizations that the United States has very often come into conflict with the Central Americans, in this sense being much better internationalists than we are because they see these organizations as a buffer against the direct application of U.S. power.

So, Nicaragua's effort to defend itself recently in the International Court of Justice in the Hague has deep roots, going back nearly eighty years in Central America, just as recent American actions in that court are almost a complete rerun of what the U.S. did in the Central American Court of Justice between 1912 and 1916.

One final note. Andrew Carnegie's court building was completed in 1917, but by then there was no longer a court to use it. Today the building houses Costa Rica's foreign ministry. It is said to be one of Carnegie's few bad investments.

I'm Bill Busenberg in Washington.

*CHAPTER 5
The Case of the Spaceman Spy
For Sherlock Holmes, it is the case of the century— perhaps the twenty-first century!

At the World Supermarket Exposition in New York, an industrial spy has attempted to steal the secret formula to a new space-age product, Cosmic Cola, a complete meal in a soda drink. The Exposition has been attended by thousands of people because the products on display include not only the latest items that are available in supermarkets, but also experimental products that may become available in the future. Among the futuristic products, Cosmic Cola has received the most attention because it is the most revolutionary and has the greatest profit-making potential.

The police are holding three suspects, all of whom claim to be U.S. citizens and all of whom were in the area of the Cosmic Cola display at the time of the attempted theft. The police have asked Mr. Holmes for assistance in questioning the suspects because of one very unusual circumstance—they believe the spy is from outer space! Just before the attempted theft, several people reported that they saw a UFO land near the exposition center and that they also saw someone get out of the UFO before it flew away again.

Holmes: Could you explain, sir, who you are and what you were doing at the time of the attempted theft?

Suspect number 1: Sure. I'm Fred Taylor from St. Paul, Minnesota, and I'm here in New York on vacation. I was trying to get to the fish farm display because the idea of raising fish in a supermarket and selling them so cheap really interested me. But the problem was I got lost, and I was walking down the aisle past the Cosmic Cola display when the police grabbed me. And that's all.

Holmes: So you're a tourist and you walked down the wrong aisle while you were trying to find the fish farm. Then the police got you. All right. And how about you— who are you and what were you doing?

Suspect number 2: I'm Robert Gordon, from Miami, Florida. I'm an insurance salesman, and I'm in New York for a business meeting in our national office. I came over to the Exposition during our lunch break, and I thought I'd try a McSushiburger, an experimental product that's a combination of Japanese sushi and American hamburger. I was just wandering around eating, and I guess I ended up in the wrong place at the wrong time.

Holmes: I see. In other words, you left your insurance meeting and came over here to eat lunch. You were looking around at things and just happened to be near the Cosmic Cola display when the trouble started. All right. And how about you?

Suspect number 3: Malcolm Landry, sir, resident of the great state of Washington. I work for the president of the United States in the field of foreign affairs, and I came down here to New York just for the day to deliver some papers to the American ambassador to the United Nations. I was on my way to buy a container of eggs, a box of milk, and a tube of bread for dinner when I dropped the eggs, slipped on the broken parts, and crashed into the Cosmic Cola display. I'm a victim of circumstances, but the police won't believe me.

Holmes: I see. If I understand you correctly, you're a diplomat from Washington "state." You came "down" here to New York "just for the day," and you were buying supermarket food for dinner—a "container" of eggs, a "box" of milk, and a "tube" of bread—and you had an accident with the eggs. All right, thank you and thanks also to the other two gentlemen. No more questions. Officer, arrest your spaceman!

Listening Skill: Summarizing—Example

Statement	Possible Summarizing Response
Mr. Brown used to teach at a school that had a lot of dogs on campus. He said that sometimes it seemed as if there were more dogs than students! And one beautiful spring day, when he held a class outside on the grass, he actually found seven dogs present and only six students!	So, for Mr. Brown, there really were more dogs than students at his old school that day! That's incredible!

Exercise 1
Statements
1. It's amazing how some places get a bad reputation: for example, New York City. There have been so many movies and TV shows showing crime and violence there that a lot of people are afraid to even visit. But it's really a great city and millions of people

like living and working there. Yes, there are some problem areas in New York, but almost every big city in the world has something like that.

2. My wife and I are very happy about a desk that we bought in a used furniture store. It's a big oak desk, very old and very well made. Like a lot of older things, it's much nicer than most of the new types that you see nowadays.

3. Let me give you some advice about how to be successful in school. First of all, it's important of course to study hard and to get work done on time. But it's also important to find time to study or pursue things that interest you personally. And another thing—make sure that you fit in some fun and relaxation. It's sad to see some people have problems because all they do is study all the time.

4. There really are different levels of understanding. For example, when you're young, you might think that you understand something well, maybe what it's like to have a child. And you do understand. But, then, when the real experience of parenthood comes along, you understand better somehow, at a much deeper level.

5. Memorable meals—most people who cook have had memorable meals, those unforgettable experiences they can tell you about, especially from the time they first started cooking. As for me, how can I ever forget my first attempt at making fried rice, Chinese style, and adding the only other ingredient I could find in the house—hot dogs? To this day, at least in my memory, I have never recovered from that once-in-a-lifetime specialty—hot dog fried rice. Yuck!

6. I've had a terrible day so far. First, my car wouldn't start, so I had to take the bus to school, and I got here late. Then I remembered that I left my lunch at home and that I didn't have enough money to buy lunch. And now I'm afraid someone has taken my umbrella, after I left it by accident in the library. What a day!

7. Someone should do a study not on the amount of violence on TV and in the movies, but on the way violence is shown. Most of it seems very unrealistic because people who are punched or shot or crashed into seem to bounce around as if very little had happened to them. Other violence is shown in a very stylized way, as if it were a form of art to be appreciated. Why can't the truth about violence be shown?

Exercise 2
Statements
1. It's easy to complain about institutional food, the kind of food you get in a school cafeteria. What happens is that people are usually comparing the food to home cooking, which is obviously very different. Many times they just like to hear themselves complain. Criticism should be more constructive, so that the food can be improved as *institutional* food, not something else.

2. Reading to children at an early age is supposed to be great for their development, but Diane and Rod wonder what they have started. Their daughter, at eight months, can barely roll around, but what she does is drink her bottle of milk by resting it on her chest—just so that her hands can be free to hold a book up in front of her face. Now that's what I call an early reader!

3. Hong is one of those people who has turned out to be completely different from the way he started and from the way people thought he would be. His parents had to literally drag him to school when it was time for him to begin first grade. Now, thirty years later; you can't get him to leave.

4. There are some things we do in life that seem to have small rewards, and only after a great deal of hard work—but still those things are worth it. Acting in a play is the example that comes to mind. It's at least 95 percent hard, hard work, and the audience's appreciation comes for only a few seconds at the end of a performance—but the fulfillment is fantastic.

5. Do opposites attract? Or do people marry people who are like themselves? Carlos and Maria fit neither extreme. As a matter of fact, they partly fit both. They look a little bit like brother and sister, although he's tall and she's short. But their personalities are very different; they're complementary. Maybe they have the best of both worlds.

6. Some schools underestimate or undervalue student involvement, or they don't know how much students care about their school. That can lead to some surprises. At one school recently, the students proposed a clean-up day in which they themselves would volunteer to clean up the whole school campus. That turned out to be a great success and showed the school administrators how much their students really cared.

7. It happens in life that we sometimes like or even love someone that we can't entirely respect. It seems a little confusing, but I guess life isn't all black and white. For example, I have a friend who sometimes expresses prejudices against certain groups of people. His prejudices, when I hear them, make me very uncomfortable. Despite that, he is a friend. He has many fine qualities, and I can't help liking him. In a way, he is a problem person for me, but one I readily accept.

Exercise 5
Mostefa and the Count—With Articles
Mostefa went to the movies last night. He saw a new movie, *Count Dracula Bites the Dust.* Because the movie was very exciting, Mostefa ate three boxes of popcorn and drank four cups of soda. After the movie, Mostefa was a little sick. He went home and got into bed immediately. He fell asleep in a little while, but he had a very bad dream—a nightmare. He dreamed that Count Dracula was very angry with him because he ate all of the popcorn and drank all of the soda in the theater. He didn't leave any

popcorn or any soda for the Count! He dreamed that Count Dracula was very, very hungry! Finally, Mostefa woke up, got out of bed, and went into the kitchen. He made some popcorn, put it and some soda on the table for Dracula, and then went back to bed.

Exercise 6
Mostefa, the American Football Kicker?—
With Articles
Mostefa is thinking about trying to become a professional football player in the U.S. He read an article in the newspaper about the many foreign-born soccer players playing American football. It said that these soccer players have a very small job. They are on the playing field for only a few seconds at a time to make special kicks. First, they kick the football to the other team to start the first half or the second half of a game. That is called a "kickoff." They also try to kick the ball between the goal posts at the ends of the field to score points for their team. If they kick successfully from a long distance, it is a "field goal"— three points for their team. If they kick successfully from a short distance—after their team moves the ball into one of the two "end zones" for six points, a "touchdown"—then they get an "extra point" for their team. After an extra point or a field goal, they also have to "kick off" to the other team.

The ten to twenty kickers who are most successful in this work earn hundreds of thousands of dollars a year. But it is a dangerous job. During the few seconds that a kicker is on the field, there is a possibility of violent contact with much bigger and stronger players. Serious injuries may result. Sure, the medical bills that also would result would be paid by the team owners or by an insurance company, but the pain would belong entirely to the kicker.

Mostefa is going to think some more about all of the possibilities before making a decision.

CHAPTER 6
The Case of the Roundabouts
Section 1
Mrs. R: How do you do, Mr. Holmes. My name is Gabriela Roundabout, though most of my friends call me "Gabby." I think they do that partly because they think I am a little gabby. I'll admit that I talk a lot. Some say that I even talk in circles, that I don't get directly to the point. Well, I'll try with you. The important thing to say first is that I have had the great good fortune to walk through life with Brigadier General Slocum Roundabout.

Holmes: In other words, you're the wife of the brigadier general.

Section 2
Mrs. R: Yes, of course. The general has just returned from serving his country overseas in what they call a "police action." He was involved with the, uh . . . with the . . . pacification of villages—with the, the . . . elimi- nation of unreliable elements in the population. That sort of thing.

Holmes: I see. If I understand you correctly, he was at war in another country, and his job was to kill the enemy and keep control of the villages.

Section 3
Mrs. R: Well, yes, that is rather a direct way of put- ting it. At any rate, at one point he was in charge of protecting the powder—that is, the gunpowder— actually, all the ammunition and weapons for our side. During that particular service, he was wounded in the . . . the . . . well, a place that made it somewhat difficult for him to sit down.

Holmes: So he was shot in the buttocks. Very well, please go on.

Section 4
Mrs. R: Yes, well, because of that and his advanced age, the general has returned home to bring down the curtain on his illustrious career and take a final bow.

Holmes: In other words, he's retiring.

Section 5
Mrs. R: Yes, but we are being allowed to pass our final years in our residence on the grounds of the military establishment.

Holmes: I see. So you're still going to live on the army base.

Section 6
Mrs. R: Yes, that's the best thing. After fifty-four years of service, the general has slowed down considerably. It's not that his wheels are grinding to a halt. It's just that they're not turning as fast or as long or as smoothly as before. Well, you know what I mean.

Holmes: I believe I do. It sounds as if his thinking is slower and maybe a little less clear.

Section 7
Mrs. R: The army doctors who have taken care of his wound say that his clock is slowly but surely winding down. In army terms, it may not be long before he answers the last roll call. The general, though, is amazing about the subject—he even jokes about it, although somewhat crudely, saying that he'll wake up some morning and find someone patting him on the face . . . with a . . . with a shovel.

Holmes: So he may not live much longer.

Section 8
Mrs. R: But he still surprises sometimes! Why, just two days ago, the old wolf caught me in our bedroom and made me bestow my feminine favors upon him. Imagine enjoying intimate relations at our age! There's still a fire burning deep down inside him!

Holmes: So he made love to you. That's wonderful. But why, Mrs. Roundabout, are you telling me all this about the general? Why have you come to see me?

Section 9

Mrs. R: Oh, dear, yes. Well, it was just that night, just then, that we were donning our finest evening wear for a gala ball to be held at the officers' club, featuring big band music from the 1930s and 40s.

Holmes: In other words, you were getting dressed for a big formal dance.

Section 10

Mrs. R: Yes. When the general interrupted our preparations in the way that he did ... well, my goodness, I needed even more time to get ready, and I was afraid that we would be late. So I asked him to help me by taking my diamond tiara into the powder room. I was going to use the mirror there to put the tiara into my hair, but by the time I made my way into the room, the tiara wasn't anywhere to be found. And the general, when I asked him about it back in the bedroom, had by then slipped into one of his "slower" moments. He hasn't been able to remember since then what he did with the tiara.

Holmes: If I understand you correctly, you asked the general to put your tiara in the "powder room"—the bathroom, that is—but he put it somewhere else and now he can't remember where.

Mrs. R: Yes, that's right. And that's why I've come to see you. The tiara is now worth well over $15,000. Can you help me find it?

Holmes: There's a good chance that I can. In fact, you may *explode* with laughter when I tell you where I think it is.

Exercise 1
Multisyllabic Verbiage
1. educational institution
2. legal profession
3. writing instrument
4. seating place
5. financial institution
6. medical profession
7. underground transportation
8. private residence
9. financial resources
10. literary artist

Exercise 2
Euphemisms
1. preowned automobile
2. little girls' room
3. correctional institution
4. capital punishment
5. unsuccessful course completion
6. follow-up assignment for the next class
7. terminate someone's employment
8. economically disadvantaged
9. below standard air quality
10. military intervention

Exercise 3
Words Direct in Meaning
1. F grade
2. die
3. spy
4. failure
5. sick
6. insult
7. ugly
8. noise
9. stink
10. pain

Exercise 4
General Words
1. vegetable
2. job
3. family member
4. transportation
5. fruit
6. store
7. clothes
8. furniture
9. color
10. animal
11. weather
12. shape
13. sickness
14. building
15. sport
16. science
17. entertainment
18. machine
19. room
20. reading material

Exercise 5
Series of Words with Different Connotations
1. job, position
2. television, boob tube
3. noisy, loud
4. work, profession
5. foreign student, international student
6. policeman, officer, cop
7. skinny, thin, slender
8. sweat, perspiration
9. quiet, shy, withdrawn
10. composition, essay
11. poor, low-income
12. child, kid, youngster
13. average, pretty good, fair
14. quit, leave, resign
15. intellectual, egghead

*CHAPTER 7
Exercise 3
Story Number One
I had a strange dream last night. I was on a space shuttle flight, and the shuttle went far off course to a planet in another galaxy. The planet had all the same life forms that we have here, but the dolphins were the highest creatures because they combined peacefulness with intelligence. And for entertainment, they didn't go to an aquarium; instead, they went to a terrarium to see the humans and other land animals.

Story Number Two
I don't want to just *see* a UFO. I want to have a close encounter of the third kind—to actually *meet* people from another planet. My hope is that they will take me back to their planet on their spaceship and that there I will see all of the people that I have known and loved and that have died. It will be a little bit like heaven. Or it will be heaven itself.

Exercise 5
A Proposal
Since peace is important for everyone, I think all of us should think about ways of preserving it. This is my own proposal for what I would like to see happen. First, I would like to see the United Nations be given far more power for maintaining peace in the world. Second, the UN would have peacekeeping forces that would begin work by going into every country with nuclear arms and removing those arms from existence. Third, the UN would have a special court of law that would listen to problems between countries and resolve those problems before any fighting could start. Last, there would be laws that would allow the other countries in the world to punish any country that would not agree to follow the court's decision or that did not follow these procedures in general.

Many people say that they can't write poetry, or that they don't know how to go about doing it. Here's a suggestion that may be helpful, at least in the beginning. Start simply by remembering some strongly felt experience. Experiences from childhood are especially rich. Then quickly write down the impressions the experience made on your senses, something about seeing, hearing, touching, smelling, or tasting, but not necessarily using those words. Next, begin writing lines with the words "I remember" followed by an impression, "I remember" followed by another impression, and so on. Finally, go back and erase all of the "I remembers" except the first one.

*CHAPTER 8

The Case of the Friendly Prank

People love Tom Comeuppance because of all of his good traits—and despite his one very bad trait. Tom is never satisfied with anything. He always finds something to complain about and wish for, and he usually complains and wishes about the same thing for a long time. Most of the time, he also ends up getting what he has been wanting, but even then he still finds something to complain about soon after. This kind of behavior sometimes drives his family and friends crazy.

Lately, Tom has been complaining about needing a car even though his family just recently helped him get his own apartment near the school he attends, the Merlin Institute of Technology (MIT). His friends also got together and bought him a ten-speed bicycle for his birthday. This is what Tom has been saying:

"I'm tired of walking and riding around so much. I need a car. I sure wish I owned that 1965 Ford Mustang that's for sale over at Bob Fisher's used-car lot."

His friends at MIT, who are studying mechanical engineering with him, are also tired—they're tired of hearing this from him so much. In fact, they can't stand it any more. They've put up with it long enough. In other words, they are simply fed up. This is the way they let him have it in the cafeteria Friday afternoon.

"'Car, car, car'—that's all we ever hear from you these days. It's really wearing thin."

"Enough already! You sound like a broken record!"

"Yeah, could you change the record, please?"

But these words didn't hurt Tom. They rolled off him like water off a duck's back. He wasn't even bothered when the same kind of thing happened at his family's house, where he went for dinner on Saturday. The members of his family are very different in their jobs and interests—his father is a crane operator, his mother is a science fiction writer, his sister is a body builder, and his brother is a magician—but they are all alike in loving Tom very

much. Even so, there is a limit to how much their love can tolerate from him. These were their words:

"Tom, you're starting to get on my nerves with all this car talk."

"You're really rubbing me the wrong way, too."

"I'll be even more honest with you—you're going to drive me to drink!"

"Tom, you know the expression, 'Every cloud has a silver lining'? For you, the expression should be, 'Every silver lining has a cloud.'"

On Sunday, Tom spent the whole day in the library. When he got back to his apartment Sunday night, he found a very big and very unusual gift waiting for him. You could have knocked him over with a feather when he saw it. There was a note attached to it that read,

"Surprise! You've been driving us up a wall. Now it's your turn. And this time, for once, don't look a gift horse in the mouth!"

Exercise 2

Idioms

1. Hold your horses, I'll be ready to leave in just a minute.

2. I'm afraid that Hideo let the cat out of the bag and now everybody knows our plans.

3. Ravi thought he was being funny, but the fact is his joke went over like a lead balloon.

4. The basketball team is on a roll. They've won their last five games.

5. Nui is all up in the air about her planned vacation in Paris.

6. I was supposed to meet a new friend for dinner last night, but she stood me up.

7. Mr. Sato says that we have to learn to get our work done on time, so he has drawn the line on late homework.

8. Amedeo got in a jam with his parents because he forgot to tell them how late he would be getting home.

9. Fahad should have known better what to say in that situation. He sure put his foot in his mouth that time.

10. Martin was a great soccer player for many years, but he's all washed up now.

11. The police strongly suspected the owner of having burned down his own store in order to collect the insurance, so they asked him to come clean with them.

12. Some salespeople have just the right touch—they can sell anyone anything.

13. Microwave ovens cook so fast that they really make cooking a breeze.

14. Her excuse for not getting her homework done was pretty wild, but it still rang true.

15. Mei-Ling got the jump on her homework and finished it a day early.

Exercise 3
Idioms
1. Mohammed didn't come to class because he's feeling under the weather.

2. Santha is great at growing plants—she really has a green thumb.

3. When her husband died, she went to pieces.

4. It's okay to be busy, but maybe you're spreading yourself too thin.

5. I haven't heard a word from you this morning. What's the matter—cat got your tongue?

6. Because of her husband's illness, Mary has become the breadwinner for their family.

7. I believed her! I thought she was serious, but of course she was only pulling my leg.

8. Anna has worked so hard for so many years that she's feeling burned out in her job.

9. With all the problems that Luis has, is it any wonder that he's got a bad case of the blues?

10. The basketball game wasn't even close. Our team got blown away.

11. On only our second date, he asked me out of the blue to marry him!

12. I knew my boss was having a bad day, but I didn't expect him to bite my head off.

13. Have you ever noticed how some people will talk your head off on the telephone?

14. People on the street who ask Mr. Lee for money aren't going to get any—they're barking up the wrong tree with him.

15. The view from the top of this mountain will take your breath away.

Exercise 5
Two-Word Verbs
1. Bill likes Judy and thinks that she likes him, so he's going to ask her out.

2. Hong wasn't ready to answer when his teacher called on him.

3. They called off the picnic because of bad weather.

4. I came across an interesting article in the newspaper about living under the ocean.

5. A former student of mine dropped by to tell me about her new job.

6. Hae Sung dropped her clothes off at the cleaner's on her way to school.

7. International and native students in the U.S. have very different backgrounds, but they usually get along very well together.

8. Holmes is getting at the facts, but he needs to investigate further.

9. He always tries to get out of washing the dishes with the excuse that he has a lot of homework.

10. She got over her illness quickly and returned to work on Monday.

11. He doesn't like to have blood samples taken, so he asked the nurse to get it over with as quickly as possible.

12. We got through the textbook just before the final exam.

13. She has trouble with math problems. Actually, her biggest problem is that she gives up too easily.

14. She has on the new sweater that she bought last week.

15. Chen's father told him that he should keep out of other people's problems.

Exercise 6
1. It's a hard class, so I'm doing extra studying to make sure that I keep up with everyone.

2. Some spectators were kicked out of the soccer stadium for fighting.

3. Please look after my things while I go get a drink of water.

4. If you look for trouble, you'll probably find it.

5. If you look out for trouble, you probably won't have any.

6. Where did I get that answer? I made it up.

7. His grandfather passed away at the age of 98.

8. She said that she wasn't feeling very well just before she passed out.

9. Their teacher put off their test until Friday.

10. Safia ran into a friend that she hadn't seen in ten years.

11. Our best player showed up at the biggest game of the year with a broken arm.

12. Susan takes after her mother in appearance and after her father in personality.

13. One of little Keiko's jobs in her house is to take out the garbage every day.

14. Jim took his mother out to dinner on her birthday.

15. The salesman offered me a good price on that old Mustang, but I had to turn him down.

*CHAPTER 9
The Case of "The Material Shade"

Mrs. S.: Mr. Holmes, my husband has entitled his poem "The Material Shade." I know it says something about his life in our country. He himself is a kind of "shade"—which in literature, as you know, can mean a spirit, a soul, a ghost, or some kind of special presence. But he is really a *trapped* spirit, a writer who is caught between the true spiritual life and a very sad material world.

Holmes: Yes, I understand, but we must look for another meaning, a concrete one, something about a hiding place for his manuscript. A "shade" can also be a shadow, or something that protects us from light or controls light. Let's keep that in mind and think about one line at a time. Please begin. Poetry should be spoken, and I would like to hear the words from you.

Mrs. S.: All right, as you wish. The first line is, "Caught between two worlds of light and darkness."

Holmes: "Caught between two worlds of light and darkness." What does that mean? Maybe something that is not completely in light or darkness, or maybe that is sometimes light and sometimes dark. Go on.

Mrs. S.: The second line is, "A homebody with no true home or body."

Holmes: "A homebody with no true home or body." In other words, I guess, a thing can't really have a home in the way a person can, but this thing stays in the home. And it doesn't have a body, a real body. Is it like a head? Please go on.

Mrs. S.: The third line is, "A spirit easily seen through and missed."

Holmes: "A spirit easily seen through and missed." In other words, something seen through but not really seen—not noticed or paid attention to. And maybe something people would miss if they didn't have it.

Mrs. S.: The fourth line is, "Cornered, stuck to the side out of the way."

Holmes: "Cornered, stuck to the side out of the way." That's easier—something in a corner, not moving, not in people's way.

Mrs. S.: The fifth line is, "Few would care to make their way without me."

Holmes: "Few would care to make their way without me." Okay, few people would want to do anything or to move anywhere without it. I think we're getting closer.

Mrs. S.: The sixth line is, "Circle to myself, I circulate still."

Holmes: "Circle to myself, I circulate still." Hmm . . . maybe something round, but what does "circulate still" mean? It circulates itself? Maybe it circulates something else without moving. Hmm . . .

Mrs. S.: The seventh line is, "Held high in place, but passed by for others."

Holmes: "Held high in place, but passed by for others." Okay, something on top of something else, like a head we said. People go by it without paying attention to it, or something passes by it, maybe through it. The "others," whatever they are, are preferred—or it may mean the thing is used for the benefit of others, most likely people.

Mrs. S.: The eighth line is, "Active, passive, without a will of my own."

Holmes: "Active, passive, without a will of my own." Sometimes it's active, sometimes it's passive, but it has no control over that.

Mrs. S.: The ninth line is, "Material shade, lighting, shadowing."

Holmes: "Material shade, lighting, shadowing." Well, there's the title. It is a *physical* shade—it both gives light and shadows light.

Mrs. S.: The last line is, "Hauntless haunter, controlled by human hands."

Holmes: "Hauntless haunter, controlled by human hands." Again, it's not really a spirit or a ghost—it is a presence of some kind—but no one is haunted by it or notices it very much. At the same time, though, people actually control it.

Mrs. S.: Mr. Holmes, what is it? Where is the manuscript hidden?

Holmes: I'm not completely sure. Let's add up all the information. First, it's a thing in the home and like a head. People see it, but don't pay much attention to it. It's in a corner, out of people's way. Yet they need it to move around or do things. It's round and something may circulate from it, pass by it, or through it. It's on top of something else. It lights and shadows. People control it . . . Aha! Of course! Well, the old light bulb just lit up for me—but how about you? Doesn't this description sound familiar?

Exercise 1
Common Similes
1. She was as busy as a bee.
2. He moves like a cat on the tennis court.
3. I'm as hungry as a horse.
4. He fought like a tiger.
5. He ate like a pig.
6. I was quiet as a church mouse.
7. She worked like a beaver.
8. He's as strong as an ox.
9. Maria watched her children like a hawk.
10. He's big, but he's as gentle as a kitten.
11. She felt like a fish out of water.
12. Anita can be as stubborn as a mule.
13. They came charging into the room like a herd of wild elephants.
14. He was as clumsy as a bull in a china closet.
15. She ran around like a chicken with its head cut off.

Exercise 3
Original Similes
1. The baby's laughter sounded like bells ringing.
2. Her worrying was like a long winter rain.
3. His explanation was as clear as an abstract painting.
4. He searched his memory like a miner digging for gold.
5. Her eyes looked like two dimming lights.
6. She thought of her father as a bank that never closes.
7. He sighed like a balloon losing its air.
8. He looks like an unmade bed.
9. She slept like a shutdown computer.
10. He thought of marriage as an unpaid bill.

Exercise 4
Original Similes
1. He woke up feeling as fresh as new-baked bread.
2. The rain in the trees sounded like a mother's whispers to her child.
3. The dog ran and jumped, like a kite rising freely into flight.
4. His complaining was like water dripping in a sink all night.
5. She lay down to sleep, like a thick fog settling over a city.
6. I lose all control sometimes, like a speeding car without brakes.
7. His words offered as much pleasure as a leftover piece of hardened candy.
8. The autumn leaves fell to earth like red and yellow strokes of paint.

9. Her coughing sounded like explosions in a coal mine.
10. He shook my hand like a diesel truck revving up to drive away.

Exercise 6
Common Metaphors
1. She is eagle-eyed.
2. Why are you pecking at your food?
3. They wolfed down their food.
4. He was a lionhearted fighter.
5. She outfoxed me in our game.
6. I wormed my way out of trouble.
7. Who's been monkeying around with the computer?
8. We snaked our way through the crowd.
9. My chess opponent played cat and mouse with me.
10. He's a tiger on the playing field and a pussycat off it.
11. The children kept buzzing in and out of the adults' party.
12. People claw their way to the top in many professions.
13. She butted into line instead of going to the end of it.
14. We can't bury our heads in the sand regarding the possibility of nuclear war.
15. The time comes when we all have to leave our family nests.

Exercise 7
Original Metaphors
1. The mountains ripened in the September sunset.
2. Her graduation day was a last hug goodbye.
3. Our English teacher conducted our voices into perfect harmony.
4. The last day of summer was a slow, sad dance.
5. Her green ideas soon dried out and turned brown.
6. The day rolled by without stopping for any passengers.
7. His sneeze was a hurricane, however brief.
8. The jazz drummer brushed circles and squares in the air.
9. He rode the last wave in his mind onto a hushed beach.
10. She believes that some TV shows are cancers on our culture.

Exercise 8
Original Metaphors
1. He chased his cold out the door.
2. Her audience licked the frosting off her speech, but left the cake.
3. The city streets were a jazz record with scratches and pits.
4. Her car's engine is humming all the wrong notes.
5. He raced around the TV dial and then stopped to collect his thoughts.
6. The summer breeze brushed a kiss across my cheek.
7. Her love for her husband was stretched, and stretched, and stretched—and then it snapped.
8. The evening stars winked one promise after another.

9. The dentist traveled the full width and length of my Grand Canyon mouth.

10. Daylight fell, face down in the dust.

*CHAPTER 10
The Case of "Who Am I?"

Section 1

It was possibly Sherlock Holmes's strangest case, stranger even than *The Case of the Spaceman Spy*. It began with a knock on his door. The visitor who entered complained of a bump on his head and said that he couldn't remember who he was. He couldn't remember much else, either.

Section 2

The visitor was a very small individual and not very strong looking. He seemed to be well over fifty years old, and his voice was weak, almost squeaky.

Section 3

He was also wearing some unusual clothes. He had on a short-sleeve red shirt and blue pants that ended high above a pair of yellow shoes. Strangest of all, he was wearing formal-looking white gloves.

Section 4

The stranger also had a funny face. There seemed to be a lot of roundness in it. He had a round nose, big round eyes, and even big round ears that were higher up on his head than what you see on most individuals.

Section 5

The stranger thought he remembered working as an actor, singer, and dancer; mostly in comedies, he thought.

Section 6

The stranger had only four fingers on each hand.

Section 7

He didn't have any identification on him. The only thing that he had in his pockets was something called the "Key to the Magic Kingdom."

Section 8

The stranger's only other possession was a watch on his left wrist. The face of the watch contained a picture of—himself.

Section 9

The stranger couldn't remember the names of any family members. But he thought he had two friends named Donald and Goofy, a girlfriend named Minnie, and a dog named Pluto.

Section 10

The stranger believed that his own first and last names began with the letter M. He also thought that he might have had a long black tail at one time. That was all he could remember.

Exercise 1
The Perils of Pauline

Pauline Patterson, a rancher's daughter, was madly in love with Ringo Slade, the most famous outlaw in the West. Last week she decided that she had to go to him as soon as possible. This was her plan:

1. Get out of her sick bed and forget about her fever and the sharp pain in her side.

2. Take her father's new wild horse, Firebreather, because it was the fastest on their ranch.

3. Cross a desert that was heavily populated with poisonous snakes.

4. Take a shortcut down a steep cliff.

5. Find shelter under a tall tree when the electrical storm that had been predicted finally struck.

6. Swim across a very fast and very strong river.

7. Avoid the other outlaws and the law officers who were trying to capture or kill Ringo.

8. Watch out for Sadie Malone, Ringo's old girlfriend, who had already stabbed two other new girlfriends.

9. Slip her hand under Ringo's pillow while he was sleeping in order to remove the gun that he uncomfortably kept there.

Unfortunately, Pauline is now in the hospital.

Exercise 2
Statements

1. Santha's crying.

2. Amedeo has over a hundred cookbooks.

3. I heard that she does very well in all her classes.

4. I see some big black clouds blowing in fast.

5. There is always a lot of snow in the Alps.

6. Martin and Anita are taking only business classes.

7. She lives in a very expensive house and drives a very expensive car.

8. You're much too skinny!

9. Dario's car has a big dent on the left side.

10. All of the students have wonderful things to say about their composition teacher, Ms. Kramer.

Exercise 3
Statements

1. There are lots of loud voices coming from next door.

2. My neighbor, Hao, is having a big sale on just about everything in his apartment.

3. The river water isn't very clear.

4. Anna has been reading a lot of magazines about new cars.

5. I haven't seen Petra with her boyfriend Christoph in a long time.

6. The photocopying machine isn't working.

7. There aren't any textbooks for my class in the bookstore.

8. My teacher asked me to visit her during her office hours, but she didn't say about what.

9. The garbage man didn't pick up the garbage today.

10. My best friend walked past me this morning without saying a word.

Listening Skill: Inferring—Example

Statement	*Possible Response*
My friend Martin needs to get a scholarship, or he'll probably have to quit school and go back home to his country. The problem is that his grades aren't very good.	It sounds as if he won't be able to get a scholarship and will probably have to go back home.

Exercise 4
Statements

1. My boss told me that if I wanted to work for our company in Japan next September, then I should have talked to him about the possibility back in March.

2. Some movies are worth paying five dollars to see. Others are worth about half that much. Tonight's movie should have gone for about twenty-five cents, or less.

3. When it's raining cats and dogs, it's raining really hard, right? Yesterday, Diane's two-year-old said that it was raining tigers and elephants.

4. Husbands sometimes refer to their wives as the "better half." Together, of course, they make a whole, but the husbands like to make this little compliment. Thomas is different—he refers to his wife as the better three-quarters.

5. They say that what goes up must come down. In that case, Pandit had better get a safety net ready for his high hopes.

6. My husband went fishing with his friends this morning. He promised me a fresh-fish dinner for tonight. A promise is a promise. Do you know any good seafood restaurants in town?

7. Anna kept talking about needing to get that old car of hers into a garage for some repairs. Well, a friend of mine called a few minutes ago to tell me that he saw her stuck this morning on the other side of the highway.

8. My cat has a bad leg. He either fell out of a tree, or he got bitten there. Of course he has been fighting a lot with the other cats in the neighborhood.

9. Ahmed told me that either he gets a good grade on the final exam or he'll fail the course. But he also told me that he hasn't studied very much.

10. Some say that it's dangerous to have too many hopes and dreams. Others say that the alternative is a very dull way of life. I lean toward excitement myself.

Exercise 5

1. Having good neighbors like the Rijos can mean a lot. You help each other out when there's a problem. There's somebody close by to talk to. We're sure going to miss them.

2. I've been saving my money either for a new car or for a big vacation of some kind. A new car would be nice, but I really haven't had a vacation in quite a while, and they say the travel rates are very low right now.

3. Makoto was saying a couple of weeks ago that he wanted to take an art class of some kind. He said that all of his work is mental and that he'd like to *make* something for a change—have a *concrete* product for his efforts. I wonder . . . he did seem to have quite a bit of paint on his hands this afternoon.

4. Roberto had been thinking about going straight into college after getting his high school diploma. A year off, though, may help him to be more ready, both financially and mentally.

5. Hard work should result in good pay, shouldn't it? Or there should be some kind of reward, if only a good word from the boss, right? Well, today, there's a line from a song that keeps going through my head: "Work your fingers to the bone, what do you get?—Bony fingers, bony fingers."

6. My father warned me that if I wanted to avoid a serious injury, then I should have accepted a basketball scholarship to Farnsworth University instead of a football scholarship to Merlin.

7. They say that one of the worst-paying professions to go into right now is teaching. But money isn't the most important thing to me.

8. If I buy a TV, I'll be able to see some of the special educational shows that I've been missing. On the other hand, watching TV can take up a lot of my time, and I don't think I want that to happen.

9. If our school's soccer team doesn't win its game on Saturday, then it will fall out of first place in the conference. The problem is that our three best players are injured and won't be able to play in the game.

10. My boss told me that there are only two ways to go in this business—either up or out. He said that he wants to talk to me some more about a career development plan in the company.

Exercise 7
One Half of a Telephone Conversation:
Conversation Number One
. . .
Oh, hi, darling, what's up?
. . .
To the doctor? How come? Is everything all right?
. . .
Well, why did you go? You didn't tell me anything about an appointment.
. . .
You wanted to be sure about what? You mean . . .
. . .
Really, are you sure?
. . .
But you didn't tell me anything—why not?
. . .
Well, yes, it's a surprise all right. I didn't think it would happen this fast.
. . .
Yeah, I know we planned on it. Now we'll have to get ready.
. . .
Well, yes, I think there is a lot to do. What's the due date?
. . .
Have you told anybody else yet?
. . .
Your parents are really going to be surprised. And mine, too.
. . .
Yeah, we should call them tonight. But let's go out and celebrate first.
. . .
That's right, we won't have much time later.
. . .
Me? I couldn't be happier, but I am starting to think about the changes this will mean and the responsibilities.
. . .
Yes, it's all part of life, and now we'll have, as they say, "a new life together."
. . .
Okay, I'll see you at home later, and then we'll go out to dinner to celebrate.
. . .
Okay, 'bye. I love you, too—and I mean T-W-O!

One Half of a Telephone Conversation:
Conversation Number Two
. . .

Hello, is this Mr. Shaver, James "Lefty" Shaver, star basketball player of the Boston Beanpoles?
. . .
This is the person who sent you the anonymous letter about your . . . uh, shall we say, your "financial problems."
. . .
Now, now, Mr. Shaver, there's no need to get angry. And it doesn't matter who I am or how I found out. Just like you, I don't want anyone else to find out about your, uh, "problems."
. . .
Yes, you're right, I do want something else also. I want you to do me a little favor every now and then in return for my helping you to keep your secret. To get right down to it, Mr. Shaver, I want you to have a strong, "positive" influence on the final score of some of the Beanpoles' basketball games.
. . .
No, Mr. Shaver, I prefer to think of my line of work as "investments." I want you to think of it as a matter of investment also. For you, it may also be a matter of insurance.
. . .
No, I don't want you to "throw" games, as you put it. We're not talking about losing anything. Far from it. I simply want you to take a "particular interest" in the points scored. There's no harm to your team in winning by 7 points instead of 3—or vice versa—now is there?
. . .
You're getting upset again, Mr. Shaver. Believe me, you have nothing to lose and everything to . . . uh, protect.
. . .
No, I don't think you want to go to the police, considering the problems you've had. Listen, I'll even make you an offer. You can gain from this arrangement also. I can help you make, uh, "investments" of your own so that you too can make a little money on the side . . .
. . .
Have it your way—as far as that goes. But let me remind you that your wife and children are also involved in this. We wouldn't want them to find out or to get hurt in any way, now would we?
. . .
There, there, Mr. Shaver, there's no need to make any threats, especially ones you couldn't possibly carry out. Believe me, you can learn to accept things, even like them. Tell me, Mr. Shaver—may I call you "Lefty"?—what do you say to my, uh, "business proposition"?
. . .
I don't know what there is to think over. I can give you a little time, but of course not too much. After all, I am in "business."
. . .
Very well, then, just a little time. You'll be hearing from me again soon. Good night, then, Mr. Shaver— "Lefty."

*CHAPTER 11
The Case of the President's Hot Seat

Hardacre: Mr. Holmes, my name is William Hardacre. I'm the new president of Meriweather University, and I have a terrible problem that I hope you can help me with.

Holmes: Very well, I'll try.

Hardacre: Well, I realize that I've caused some pain on campus, but I didn't think I had created any grounds for threats or violence. This is what has happened. During the past two weeks, three letters have appeared out of nowhere on my office desk. I have sat down and opened them, and each time I have found a note telling me to quit my job. Much worse, I have also found each time a photograph of a doll looking like me with first one, then two, and most recently three needles stuck in its buttocks. At the very same moment, I have experienced a terrible sharp pain in the same part of my body. A worse pain each time.

Holmes: Yes, I see, a case of returning a pain in the, as you say, "buttocks." Do you have any idea why you are receiving these letters?

Hardacre: No, not exactly. Well, I know I'm not a popular president. Among other things, I've had to make some tough decisions because of all the financial trouble the university is in. I've even been accused of practicing "voodoo economics."

Holmes: You mean following economic policies that seem to be based more on wishes for some kind of magical cure than on realistic thinking.

Hardacre: Yes, of course, although I obviously don't see it that way myself. Now, my latest proposal has created the biggest uproar of all. I've proposed that the university raise students' tuition by one-third and also cut the salaries of teachers and staff by the same amount.

Holmes: I can see where you're not very popular. Mr. Hardacre . . .

Hardacre: *President* . . .

Holmes: Excuse me, *President* Hardacre, could you tell me who was in your office on the day you received your most recent hate letter?

Hardacre: I think there were only four people who came in before I found the letter around noon. Jim Rainberry, the head of maintenance on campus, was in at 10:00 to review maintenance needs and what they'd cost. I also got him to do some work on the air conditioner behind my desk that I've been having trouble with.

Holmes: Please go on. Who else?

Hardacre: Well, at 10:30 I had a meeting with Lawrence Grapesun. He's a professor of electrical engineering and also the chairman of the teacher and staff union on campus. He wanted to express the union's concerns regarding my proposed cut in salaries.

Holmes: After that?

Hardacre: Well, Melanie Snowden, the cafeteria manager, brought my lunch over at 11:30, as she usually does, so that I can keep working at my desk. Then Windy Peartree, my secretary, brought me a cup of coffee from the outer office around 11:45. And that's all.

Holmes: Very good. I'm beginning to get the picture.

Hardacre: Mr. Holmes, I am not a superstitious man by nature, and I don't like the idea of being forced to quit, but it seems to me that strange forces are at work—forces that are out to get me. Here, see for yourself what was written across yesterday's photograph—"This is for the voodoo you do!"

Holmes: Yes, I see. I will need to make some more inquiries, but don't worry. I think we can get you out of—how shall I put it?—the "hot seat" you've been in.

Exercise 1
Riddles
1. What vegetable is the opposite of war?

2. What fruit is a color?

3. What vegetable is like a telephoning plant?

4. What vegetable makes a suggestion for our group?

5. What hot vegetable describes cold weather?

6. What vegetable is like a weekly paycheck?

Exercise 5
Anagram Words

1. name	9. seat
2. read	10. team
3. note	11. lead
4. part	12. dogs
5. lamp	13. race
6. ring	14. face
7. kiss	15. quiet
8. evil	

Exercise 6
Multiplication Words

1. father	4. nature
2. sidewalk	5. handsome
3. birthday	

Exercise 7
Word Groups
1. basketball, soccer, swimming, skiing, volleyball

2. red, blue, white, orange, green

3. mother, sister, uncle, grandfather, cousin

4. radio, newspaper, television, magazine

5. rock 'n' roll, opera, jazz, classical, pop

6. repeating, summarizing, guessing, paraphrasing, inferring

7. milk, orange juice, coffee, water, soda

8. monkeys, elephants, turtles, bears, parrots

9. wind, sun, rain, cold, snow

10. excellent, fine, good, wonderful, great

11. happy, angry, sad, proud, worried

12. ring, bracelet, earrings, pin, necklace

Exercise 8
Word Groups
1. shirt, socks, shoes, apple, pants

2. house, library, skyscraper, watch, church

3. poem, baby, story, essay, biography

4. lunch, year, second, week, hour

5. cake, mother, ice cream, cookies, pie

6. chemistry, biology, art, geology, physics

7. kitchen, park, bedroom, bathroom, living room

8. river, lake, ocean, hill, sea

9. computer, typewriter, photocopier, calculator, dictionary

10. carrots, potatoes, peas, lettuce, grapes

11. nose, foot, ear, eye, cheek

12. bears, humans, turtles, rabbits, whales

*CHAPTER 12
The Case of the Green Eyes, or "Isle Be Seeing You"

Harriet Beechcroft, a wealthy London socialite, has had a doubly awful experience. Her new boyfriend, Georgie Drummond, and her Emerald Isle Earrings have disappeared at the same time. The earrings are two precious emeralds shaped like the island country of Ireland and valued together at $250,000.

Police records show that Drummond, real name Willie Filcher, has a long history of theft. However, when the police went to arrest him and search his apartment for the earrings, they found that he was gone and that his apartment had been broken into. Clothes, books, and papers were scattered all over the floor. Furniture was knocked over and thrown about. Chairs, pillows, and the bed were ripped open and the insides torn out. From the looks of it, Drummond had cheated his partners in crime, and they had come looking for him and the earrings. He was unlikely to return as a result.

At Sherlock Holmes's insistence, he and Ms. Beechcroft have gone to the apartment to have a look around. There Holmes finds two clues that both the criminals and the police overlooked. First, the Miss Lonelyhearts section of yesterday's *London Telegraph* newspaper had been circled and the name "Emma" written on the side. Second, a photograph in Drummond's bedroom reveals "Emma" to be Emma Raleigh, his true love.

Holmes: I'm sorry that Drummond has broken your heart, Ms. Beechcroft. But I think we have a chance of getting back your earrings. My guess is that Drummond has hidden them for safekeeping. He's in hiding himself and doesn't even dare use the usual methods to communicate with someone about the earrings. He believes that total secrecy is his only choice. Why else would he write the name of the person he's in love with next to Miss Lonelyhearts, the section of the paper that's for people hopelessly out of love?

Beechcroft: What do you mean, Mr. Holmes?

Holmes: I mean that if we read the letters to Miss Lonelyhearts in tomorrow's paper, we will find out where your earrings are hidden.

The Miss Lonelyhearts section the next day contains only the following letter:

Dear Miss Lonelyhearts:

I'm looking for a woman who will help me change my life. She should be distantly attractive, coolly inviting, mysteriously green-eyed—all like a cat. I would also like someone whose hair is strawberry blonde, a hot and cool color at the same time. That is my dream woman in terms of appearance. In terms of personality, she should be the kind of person who won't get into any trouble or get me into any trouble. I don't want to end up in a jam again, where too many other women have led me before.

I'm so desperate to meet this dream woman that I'll even list my telephone number in the paper, just so that she can call me: 293-9690.

As for me, I'm handsome, intelligent, and wealthy—a jewel of a guy. Please call.

Isle be seeing you,
GD

Beechcroft: Mr. Holmes, this letter doesn't tell us anything, does it? Oh, all I can think about is how much I hate him and especially that Emma, whoever she is!

Holmes: You'll have to slay that green-eyed monster by the name of jealousy, Ms. Beechcroft. And the best way to do that in this case is to turn the tables and steal back the earrings. That way you'll turn GD and

Emma completely green—not with emeralds or money, but with envy. Come along. It's time to get back at those two—by getting back your earrings!

Exercise 1
Homonyms

1. sale + sail
2. hi + high
3. no + know
4. meet + meat
5. sun + son
6. new + knew
7. ate + eight
8. steal + steel
9. mail + male
10. hole + whole
11. break + brake
12. plane + plain
13. soul + sole
14. tale + tail
15. a head + ahead

Exercise 3
Word Play in Sentences

1. There was so much *snow* on our TV screen that the repairperson had to use a shovel to fix it.
2. Poor Miss Lonelyhearts—the only *male* companionship she gets is from the letter carrier.
3. A woman in line at the supermarket asked if she could go *by* me, so I had to tell her I wasn't for sale.
4. A *lead* pencil will show you the *right* way.
5. When he asked, "What's *up*?" I responded, "*Hi*!"
6. Anna thought she had caught a cold, but then it *flu*.
7. Is it true that all soccer players reach their *goals* in life?
8. A shoplifter who has second thoughts about his crime will most likely *restore* a business.
9. Instead of a new king *reigning*, the people had hoped for a long dry spell.
10. Dr. Frankenstein is ambitious and would like to get *ahead*, but his assistant likes the one he already has.

Exercise 4
Word Play in Sentences

1. They think so highly of their bright young *son* that you would think he never sets.
2. The *run* in her nylons turned into a marathon.
3. That guy used to be a dirty fighter, but now he's *all washed up.*
4. Old war movies just *kill* me.
5. The students wanted to take a *break*—but their teacher *drove* them even harder.
6. He *steeled* himself for a bad situation—no one could find him anywhere.
7. After she *dyed* her hair last night, her boyfriend went into *mourning.*
8. Mr. Morton never laughs—in fact, he's so *grave* that they almost buried him once.
9. A bum went into a bank for *a loan*, so naturally everyone walked away from him.
10. He worked so hard to *cook up* a great pun that it came out *overdone.*

Exercise 6
Poem

Living Tenderly

My body a rounded stone
with a pattern of smooth seams.
My head a short snake,
retractive, projective.
My legs come out of their sleeves
or shrink within,
and so does my chin.
My eyelids are quick clamps.
My back is my roof.
I am always at home.
I travel where my house walks.
It is a smooth stone.
It floats within the lake,
or rests in the dust.
My flesh lives tenderly
inside its bone.

Metaphors

I'm a riddle in nine syllables,
An elephant, a ponderous house,
A melon strolling on two tendrils.
O red fruit, ivory, fine timbers!
This loaf's big with its yeasty rising.
Money's new-minted in this fat purse.
I'm a means, a stage, a cow in calf.
I've eaten a bag of green apples,
Boarded the train there's no getting off.

A Parable

A man traveling across a field suddenly met a tiger. He ran away, and the tiger chased after him. Coming to a cliff, the man caught hold of a wild vine and swung himself down over the edge. The tiger sniffed at him from above. Shaking, the man looked down and saw, far below, another tiger waiting to eat him. Only the vine kept him from falling.

Two mice, one white and one black, started to eat through the vine little by little. The man saw a luscious strawberry near him. Grasping the vine with one hand, he plucked the strawberry with the other. How sweet it tasted!

*CHAPTER 13
A Case of Spirits
Holmes: Watson, there's somebody ringing the doorbell downstairs. Please bring the person up.

Watson: Very well, Holmes, but who could be calling on us at this time of night?

Holmes: Someone in great trouble, by the sound of it. Hurry along, please, and bring him up.

* * * * * * * *

Visitor: Mr. Holmes, you've got to help me! I want to call the whole thing off immediately. I'll do anything to get out of this, this . . .

Holmes: Situation? Yes, I understand. But first calm yourself and pick your story up at the beginning, please.

Visitor: Well, it's like this. When I got out of work this evening, I decided to get into the holiday spirit by stopping at Casey's Bar for a couple of . . . well, you know . . .

Holmes: A couple of drinks. Yes, I see, the "holiday spirit." Well, what then?

Visitor: Well, to be honest, a couple turned into a few too many. When I left the bar, I didn't want to run into any trouble, so I was looking out for the uh, the, uh . . .

Holmes: Police. Yes, I understand. And then?

Visitor: And then . . . well, it was then that I . . . I . . . I came across a . . . a . . . spirit.

Holmes: A spirit?

Visitor: Yes, a spirit. Well, I don't believe in spirits ordinarily, so I told the thing to take off. But it wouldn't. So I said, "Look, spirit, don't try to put any funny stuff over on me. I know what you want, and I simply have to turn you down this time because I'm not ready to . . . to . . .

Holmes: Die? Yes, yes, go on.

Visitor: Well, that's when I made a bad mistake and got myself into even worse trouble. I don't know why, but I made a bet with the spirit! I told it that I was taking off, and I bet that it couldn't keep up with me. But the faster I ran . . .

Holmes: The faster it ran, too. All along the glass store fronts downtown.

Visitor: Why, yes, how did you know?

Holmes: It's elementary, my dear fellow.

Visitor: But can you help me somehow? I'm afraid, really afraid that it's going to catch up with me and take me . . . take me . . .

Holmes: Away? Not on your life, my good man. Go back downstairs and take a good look at one of the store windows. You'll soon figure out that the only spirits after you are the ones that you've been . . .

Listening Skill: Anticipating—Example

Statement	Possible Response
It's amazing. You know what I'm going to say before I even s . . .	Say it.

Exercise 1
Statements
1. Elephants are my favorite animals at the z . . .
2. I'm glad that I don't have any classes on Friday a . . .
3. Many people don't have time in the morning for br . . .
4. Their little girl is very pre . . .
5. Climb one step at a time and don't look d . . .
6. Jae Kon needs to get his car f . . .
7. Martha had to rush home because of an e . . .
8. It's time to take the pizza out of the o . . .
9. Turn here—that house over there is m . . .
10. There are many ways to respond to your qu . . .
11. Mrs. Soto's doctor told her to quit sm . . .
12. They exercise three nights a week in the g . . .
13. It's really raining hard. Can I borrow your um . . .
14. It's impossible to get a room at some hotels without a r . . .
15. People used to consider the idea of traveling in outer space to be im . . .

Exercise 2
Song

I'm being swallowed by a boa constrictor,	O no, O no, he's up to my toes—up to my . . .
I'm being swallowed by a boa constrictor,	O gee, O gee, he's up to my . . .
I'm being swallowed by a boa constrictor,	O fiddle, O fiddle, he's up to my . . .
And I don't like it very much.	O heck, O heck, he's up to my . . .
	O dread, O dread, he's up to my (pffft)!

©

Exercise 3
Statements
1. I paid for it, so it belongs . . .
2. They started picking apples at 9:00, and they've picked over 300 . . .
3. You have a simple choice for this course— either you study hard or . . .
4. Chicago is a big city, but New York . . .
5. Naoko, I would find a better place to study if I . . .
6. He borrowed the new bestselling book from the library instead of going to a bookstore and . . .
7. The more she tried, the less . . .
8. We don't want to buy all of the package—we only want . . .
9. Toi Yee didn't feel well during the performance, but she felt . . .
10. A car dealer cheated me once in my life, and no other dealer . . .
11. Like most people, I go to the beach to sunbathe and . . .
12. Khalil would rather sleep late than . . .
13. There is a lot of joy with one son or daughter, and with two . . .
14. He talks slowly, but he thinks . . .
15. Ok Sil works a lot of late hours as a taxi driver, so naturally she saw the UFO while . . .

200   Build Your Case

Exercise 4

Statements

1. The important thing about education is not just getting it. What's really important is . . .

2. Machines won't create great problems with unemployment because we will always need people to . . .

3. Akira jokes about drinking coffee. He calls it "rocket fuel." After he has had a cup, he . . .

4. It is often difficult to accept the death of a loved one. Even weeks or months afterwards, it's common for a person to dream that . . .

5. Some restaurants have requirements about the way customers should dress. For example, I tried going into one place with a jacket but no tie, and . . .

6. The idea of a human being flying completely under his or her own power was once a dream, and then it seemed an impossibility. But a few years ago . . .

7. House plants can fool you sometimes. It might seem that they're dying or even completely dead, but then . . .

8. When people think of competition, they usually think of competing against *other* people. Well, the most challenging and meaningful competition is really . . .

9. I paid $125 to get my car ready for the winter. So, what happened? I ran out to my car this morning to go to work, and . . .

10. Little children are very interesting. Sometimes you don't know if they understand what you tell them—like a new word, for example. Then, two or three days later . . .

Exercise 5

Statements

1. For most people, no matter how much they enjoy eating out at restaurants, after a while, they . . .

2. Quite a few wise people over the years have said that peace doesn't begin with countries or even with small groups. It begins . . .

3. Reading to children at home has proven to be very, very important for their educational development. When those children begin school, they . . .

4. The first day after a marathon race, runners don't feel too bad, but the second day after . . .

5. I knew this crazy guy who, during one semester, took all his notes for a course in a circle that kept getting smaller and smaller! Well, of course, when it came time to prepare for the final exam, he . . .

6. Many people in the U.S. move from one part of the country to another—often several times—because of job considerations. The effect that this has on their extended family, naturally enough, is that . . .

7. I have a difficult time waking up in the morning. This causes problems when I'm getting dressed. Sometimes when I get to work, I look down at my shoes or socks and find out to my embarrassment that . . .

8. Telling someone what to do, or how to do something, can be a little frustrating sometimes. You explain very carefully, over and over again, and the person still . . .

9. I haven't had a TV set for a long time. When I went over to a friend's house to watch some television the other day, I didn't even know how to . . .

10. My wife had a job interview last Friday. She wasn't sure if she was really interested in the job at first, but the more she learned about it, the more interested she became. Well, she was very happy this morning when the telephone rang and . . .

*CHAPTER 14
The Case of the Cheap Déjà Vu

Section 1

Flake: How do you do, Mr. Holmes. My name is Fulton Flake. I am a professor of, uh, of economics at Farnsworth University. Well, now, let me get straight to the point, at least, that is, as best as I can. The fact is that no psychologist has been able to help me, and I thought that a famous detective like yourself might. Actually, my problem seems to be in two parts. First of all, I seem to forget many, many things. At the same time, however—and this is the second part of my problem—I have a sense that a lot of my experiences have happened before. For example, right now, *here*, I have a sense of . . . of . . .

Holmes: Of having been here before? Of a déjà vu experience, in other words?

Section 2

Flake: Why, yes, a sense that I've already met you and talked about this . . . this . . .

Holmes: Problem. Yes, it definitely is a problem. And it's one that I believe would be best for *you* to solve, with my help.

Section 3

Flake: Well, I don't know how *I* can solve it. My time is so taken up with teaching and my students and so many other things that I . . . I . . .

Holmes: Don't have time for anything else? Don't know where to begin? You're too busy? Yes, I think that that is part of the problem. You get so deeply involved in your work that you lose track of other things, including your own life.

Section 4

Flake: I'm afraid you're right there. My wife even says that I would lose my head if it weren't screwed on so tight. She says that the only thing I don't forget is *money*—that otherwise I am a classic case of the . . . the . . .

Holmes: Absent-minded professor? Forgetful person? Yes, I think so. I would advise you to give more time and attention to your private life.

Section 5

Flake: Just a minute! See, there it is, happening again. I may forget a lot, but I also have this special sense of living some experiences twice. I remember your saying those same exact words to me once before even though we have never . . . never . . .

Holmes: Met before? Seen each other before? Think *very* carefully.

Section 6

Flake: Well, it almost seems as if I just saw you yesterday, as if I sat in this same chair, as if I heard from you the same . . . the same . . .

Holmes: Advice? The same words? And what if you actually *had* been here yesterday and we actually *had* done all this before?

Section 7

Flake: Oh, really . . . well, uh, in that case, uh, would I, uh, would I have to, uh, pay more than *once*?—even though the advice is the, uh . . . is the, uh . . .

Holmes: The same? Why, yes, of course.

Section 8

Flake: Well, in that case, I'm afraid, you can just . . . you can just . . .

Holmes: Forget it? Let it go by? Sorry, Professor, *I* cannot. Especially since this is not the *second* time you've been here, but *actually* . . .

Exercise 1
Different Emphases

1. *Mary* swam across the river.
2. Mary *swam* across the river.
3. Mary swam *across* the river.
4. Mary swam across the *river*.
5. Mary swam across *the* river.

Exercise 3
Different Attitudes

1. Mary swam across the river. (unbelieving)
2. Mary swam across the river. (angry)
3. Mary swam across the river. (proud)
4. Mary swam across the river. (unimpressed)
5. Mary swam across the river. (excited)

Exercise 6
Things That Hold Some Promise

1. A school bell ringing
2. Being rubbed by a cat
3. Air turning brown over a city
4. Traveling to a foreign country
5. A pencil grinding in a pencil sharpener
6. Buying a present for someone
7. A steaming cup of hot coffee
8. A full moon rising
9. The telephone ringing in the middle of the night
10. Going to a party or being with friends

*CHAPTER 15
The Case of Life or Death

It is the year 2395. Sherlock Holmes XIII, the Great Cosmic Unraveler, has led an evacuation of people from the expended planet Earth to the only other known planet in the universe that can support human life. That planet is called Htrae. Unfortunately, the inhabitants of Htrae, the Oge Retla, have suffered terribly as a result of the Earth people's coming. As a matter of fact, war and disease brought by the Earth people have finally killed all of the Oge Retla.

The Oge Retla themselves had come to Htrae centuries before from their own expended planet and had replaced an earlier civilization also. Their history was thus very similar to the Earth people's. Actually, their entire way of being was very similar. They were very ambitious, very competitive, and very individualistic—to the point of being selfish. At the same time, they had some understanding and some compassion for others, too.

The Oge Retla knew their history well, and they generally understood themselves historically in relation to others. They knew that their civilization, like others before it, could not continue forever. They had made great advances, but they expected others to make even greater advances after them. They had surpassed others, and still others would likely surpass them.

However, the Oge Retla knew these things mostly in an intellectual way. Emotionally, they were still very undeveloped. In particular, they had a great deal of pride. They felt that their civilization was the greatest civilization ever. They felt that they could and should continue to be the greatest ever. They were frustrated, angry, and bitter when they failed to come in first in anything.

Thus it was that intellectually they generally understood and accepted their fate at the hands of the Earth people. Emotionally, however, it was a different story. Their pride made it very difficult for them to feel any understanding or acceptance of the Earth people and what they had done. As a result, in their last days, the Oge Retla were left with a greatly ambivalent attitude toward the Earth people and the future, a future without any Oge Retla. Their thoughts and feelings were greatly tangled, greatly mixed.

It is those thoughts and feelings, indeed, that Sherlock Holmes XIII, the Great Cosmic Unraveler, has to unravel as finely as possible. It is absolutely necessary for him to do so because the Oge Retla left behind two great vaults, inside one of which is the nuclear fuel that the Earth people need. In a word, that vault contains life. Inside the other vault is the nuclear waste that could contaminate all of Htrae and kill all of the Earth people. That vault, if opened, is death.

The Oge Retla left behind a message that the vault at the *north* pole of Htrae, not the vault at the *south* pole, should be opened. The question Holmes XIII has to answer is this: What is inside the north-pole vault? Nuclear fuel or nuclear waste? Life or death?

Listening Skill: Evaluating—Example

Statement

Shoplifting isn't so bad if you really need something—like something for your family—and you don't have the money for it. After all, you're stealing from a big business, not an individual, and big businesses do their own kind of stealing from us all the time.

Possible Responses

1. Well, that may be what you think. For me, it's still stealing, which is wrong in any situation.

2. I see what you're saying, but stealing like that can still end up hurting someone—employees for the company getting less pay because of smaller profits, other consumers paying more for things for the same reason, even you yourself because of the way you end up thinking about yourself.

3. I agree with you, but only in very special circumstances.

Exercise 1

Statements Dealing with Ethics

1. It's a person's responsibility to report anyone that he or she sees shoplifting.

2. Some people on the streets in big cities ask for "spare change," like twenty-five cents. It's a good idea to give it to them if you can.

3. If there's a long line of people waiting for something and you're in too much of a hurry to go to the end of the line, it's okay to go to the front ahead of the other people.

4. It's not right to complain about one friend to another friend, or to criticize one co-worker in a conversation you're having with another co-worker.

5. If you really need the help, it's okay to have someone do your homework for you.

6. There's nothing wrong with laughing at someone who makes a really stupid mistake.

7. If your grandparents give you some wrong advice, you should tell them so, just as you would tell anyone else.

8. If a classmate wants to cheat in school, that's his or her business as long as he or she doesn't try to cheat from you.

9. If a cashier in a store gives you back too much change and you keep it, that's not stealing—that's just his or her mistake.

10. Being nice to someone only because you want something from him or her is understood and acceptable behavior.

Exercise 2

Statements Dealing with Ethics

1. If someone treats you badly, you have every right to treat that person badly in return.

2. Sometimes it's better not to tell a loved one about something bad that you've done.

3. If two of your friends get into an angry argument, it's better not to get involved than to try to help them solve their problem.

4. It's better to lie than to tell the truth if the truth will only hurt someone's feelings.

5. If a friend or loved one cooks for you, you have no right to say anything negative about the food.

6. There's no obligation to give up your seat on a bus or subway to an old man or woman.

7. It's okay to drive faster than the speed limit if you're in a hurry, because everyone else does.

8. It's better to kill than to be killed.

9. It's not important to take only a fair share of something—for example, cake at a party—if there are a lot of other people who won't do the same.

10. It's our duty as citizens to know about the actions and policies of our governments and to take appropriate action against them if we believe they are wrong.

Exercise 4

Advertising Statements

1. Four out of five dentists recommend Galaxy toothpaste for cleaner, brighter teeth.

2. World-famous singer Julio Iglesias knows a good tune when he hears one. And for him, nothing hums along better than a Valencia automobile.

3. We can't guarantee a beautiful woman when you purchase a Casanova car—but we can guarantee sexy looks.

4. Housewife Helen Kaboodle tested the leading cat cleaners, and she found new, improved Spiffo to be the spiffiest.

5. Huggy Bear is the toy that children everywhere have been waiting for. Has he hugged your child today?

6. Oralfix cigarettes won't take your breath away—they're simply the best tasting low-tar cigarette.

7. Sour and Scour, the lemon-fresh all-purpose cleaner, simply does the job.

8. Talko translation machines help make traveling abroad a breeze.

9. Among the leading personal computers, Contron will accompany you anywhere.

10. People's telephone rings true for you.

*CHAPTER 16
The Case of Life or LIFE
Section 1

There is not much time left for the few remaining Oge Retla. Soon you Earth people will have killed us all. It is a terrible, terrible thing that you have done to us. We feel so much hate and so much desire for revenge against you.

Section 2

Why should we care anything about you Earth people? Why should we care anything about the future? There is no future for us. For us, the world is over. It might as well be over for you, too.

Section 3

We realize that you had to come to Htrae for your survival. We resisted your coming because we knew that Earth people and the Oge Retla could not survive together on this planet. We lost that war against you, which increased the rate of our destruction. The diseases that you brought and that we had no protection against would have killed us more slowly. You are not to be blamed entirely for what happened—you did what you had to do.

Section 4

We had done the same before you. We too had to come to Htrae for our survival after we had expended all of the resources on our own native planet. Our coming caused the destruction of the original inhabitants of this planet, the Htraens. Now it is our turn to pass into memory—your memory. That is the way of time and change.

Section 5

Our situation now in relation to you is in some ways similar to the situation of the United States and the Soviet Union on your planet Earth centuries ago. If one of those countries had been crazy enough to launch a nuclear attack against the other, what would have been the purpose of attacking in return? To ensure that the people of the other country would die also? To ensure the death of everyone?

Section 6

You and we are very similar. We have the same biology, the same human forms, the same way of being. And even if we were more different, we would still share life. If we could kill you, would it not be like killing ourselves?

Section 7

Yes, we are very alike—maybe too much alike. We Oge Retla are dying, but you Earth people are dying also, only more slowly. We both expended our original planets needlessly, and now this planet is being expended also. Maybe the fact is that neither of us really knows how to live. Maybe it would be better for both of us to die quickly.

Section 8

If you continued to live and then finished expending this planet also, what would you do next? Try to find another planet somewhere else in the universe? Go through the same wasteful process all over again? And then again? There are almost surely other life forms in the universe, forms that must be much less destructive. Perhaps they deserve to populate the universe, and your kind and our kind deserve to die.

Section 9

Thinking about other life forms, however, is still guesswork. And perhaps there is still time for change. Earth people have made tremendous changes, tremendous advances since their beginning. Most of those advances have occurred in the physical world through science and technology. Maybe other advances can be made also. If you open the vault containing nuclear waste, that will be certain death for you. And if you open the vault containing nuclear fuel, which produces nuclear waste, what will the ultimate result of that be? You need to think carefully about yourselves, this planet, and the changes you need to make.

Section 10

Should your minds or your hearts rule your decisions? Perhaps like us you have relied too much on thinking, or on one kind of thinking, in making advances mostly in the physical world. There has been a lack of feeling or caring in your thinking. Or maybe there has been too much feeling of a selfish kind, not enough thought about other feelings. The question you are faced with is this: Should you open the north-pole vault? You should *know in your heart* and *feel in your mind* the right thing to do. After all, you do not wish to follow us, do you?

Exercise 4
Words and Phrases for Free Association

1. happiness
2. job
3. future
4. need
5. spirit
6. want
7. family
8. activity
9. must have
10. success
11. love
12. ambition
13. care about
14. wish for
15. freedom to
16. respect
17. learn
18. give
19. nature
20. achieve
21. other people
22. yourself
23. share
24. admire
25. responsibility
26. your strongest desire
27. your strongest need
28. death
29. life
30. people's view of you—after you die

Exercise 6

Statements about Barbara

1. Barbara comes across as a very *quiet* person. In fact, she's so quiet that it's easy to overlook her.

2. However, overlooking her would be a mistake. She's not quiet because she's shy, but because she's very serious, very thoughtful. When she has something to say, it's something very worthwhile.

3. One could complain, however, that she is perhaps a bit too deliberate. A lot of good ideas can come about from being more spontaneous on occasion.

4. One would also think that because Barbara is so quiet, so deliberate, and really so intelligent, she would also be very easygoing. The fact is that she's just the opposite. She's not a very accepting person, and she ends up worrying too much.

5. But all her worrying is a sign of yet another good quality. She worries about things outside herself. She's a selfless, caring person. She cares about other people—and not just those close to her. Her goal is to be helpful to many people, and in her own quiet way she's very successful at that.

Solutions

1. *The Case of the Treasure Hunt, or "The Secret to Success"*—The treasure is hidden in the Fountain of Life, but the nature of the treasure is open to interpretation. The suggestion is that it is a philosphical treasure because of its placement in the Fountain of Life in the center of the common, surrounded by several things that reflect important aspects of life.

2. *The Case of Hitting Rockbottom*—The gardener is the guilty person. The gardener planted only two flowers in three and a half hours because he or she needed time to plan and carry out the practical joke on Mr. Rockbottom.

3. *The Case of the Missing Bracelet*—The secret message is, "BRACELET INSIDE ME." (In order to find the message in Pettibone's coded note, BIRNASCIEDLEEMTE, arrange all of the letters that are in the odd-numbered positions so that they come one after the other, and follow that with all of the letters in the even-numbered positions.) Pettibone chose this hiding place because he knew he was about to get caught and because he wanted to hide and keep the bracelet at the same time. Unfortunately, the bracelet later formed an obstruction in his body and helped cause his death.

Answers to exercise 2—Directions to Places, page 26.
1. The Trade Center is at H8.
2. The Strand movie theater is at M5.
3. The Stardust Cafe is at M2.
4. The new French bakery is at D11.
5. Contron Computer Corporation is at C6.

4. *The Case of "Why Is Today a Special Day?"*—Today is a special day for the Smith family at 2352 Northwest Cornell Street in Waterbury because their ticket in the lottery, number 2352, won a lot of money for them.

5. *The Case of the Spaceman Spy*—The spaceman spy is Malcolm Landry, the third suspect, as he inadvertently reveals in his response to Sherlock Holmes's questioning. He says that he resides in the state of Washington, but works for the President in the field of foreign affairs—that would be a long commute, to Washington, D.C. He also says that he came "down" to New York—New York is commonly said to be "up" (north) from Washington,

D.C. It is also very unusual for a high-level diplomat to buy supermarket food for dinner on a day visit to New York instead of going to a restaurant. Moreover, he makes three errors in his use of partitives related to food: a "container" instead of a carton of eggs (or a dozen eggs), a "box" instead of a quart or some other size of milk (possibly a carton also), and a "tube" instead of a loaf of bread. His flat, unaccented way of speaking is also a major tip-off. Finally, his crashing into the Cosmic Cola display is rather suspicious, to say the least.

6. *The Case of the Roundabouts*—The general, having slipped into one of his "slower moments," took his wife's diamond tiara to the wrong powder room—not to their bathroom, but to the gunpowder storage room on the army base. That is why Holmes says that Mrs. Roundabout may "*explode* with laughter" when he tells her where he thinks the tiara is.

7. *The Case of Marooned on the Moon*—The one employee who is not identified as receiving a reward is the lawyer. That suggests that he or she is the unidentified employee whom Pennypacker has fired because of "work problems." In addition, the lawyer was the last person to see Pennypacker, at 5:30 p.m. The lawyer is the guilty person.

8. *The Case of the Friendly Prank*—The "gift horse" in Tom's apartment is the 1965 Ford Mustang (a mustang is a kind of horse) that he has been wanting. The question of who put it there and how is open to speculation. His friends and family working together and using their individual areas of expertise may be the best possibility.

9. *The Case of "The Material Shade"*—The manuscript is hidden in a lampshade, possibly written in invisible ink or on microfilm. That is why Holmes says that "the old light bulb just lit up for me"—he has a bright idea about the manuscript's location and he suggests that location at the same time.

Solution to exercise 11—Discussion: Seeing in Different Ways, page 96.

Some people see a young, upper-class, and attractive woman first. Other people see an older, lower-class, and unattractive woman first. The young woman looks away from us to the left—we see mostly her left ear, cheek, and jaw and only one eyelash and the tip of her nose. The older woman also looks to the left, but a little down and a little bit towards us. Her eye is the young woman's ear, her nose is the young woman's cheek and jaw, her mouth is the young woman's neckband or necklace, and her chin is the young woman's upper chest.

10. *The Case of "Who Am I?"*—The mysterious visitor is Mickey Mouse, who apparently has suffered some loss of memory because of an injury to his head.

11. *The Case of the President's Hot Seat*—The information in the case suggests that all four of President Hardacre's visitors on the day of his most recent "voodoo" threat and attack are the perpetrators: Jim *Rainberry* (weather and fruit), Lawrence *Grapesun* (fruit and weather), *Melanie* (the same pronunciation as *melon*, a fruit) *Snow*den (weather), and *Windy* (weather) *Pear*tree (fruit). They all had motives, they are friends, and they apparently worked together in terrorizing Hardacre. Peartree has studied voodooism (a primitive religion of the West Indies), Snowden made the voodoo doll and took the photographs, Rainberry wired electricity from the "faulty" air conditioner to the President's chair, and Grapesun engineered and used the remote-control device that gave the President electric shocks in his chair. The President was in a "hot seat" because he was both in a lot of trouble and in an electrified chair.

12. *The Case of the Green Eyes, or "Isle Be Seeing You"*—The telephone number in GD's letter to Miss Lonelyhearts points to the words that, when combined, indicate the hiding place of the stolen earrings. The odd order of digits (first, third, and fifth) indicate the key sentences in the letter, and the even order of digits (second, fourth, and sixth) indicate the key words in those sentences (the last digit, 0, naturally indicates nothing). The resulting message is "green-eyed strawbery jam," which suggests that Drummond hid the earrings in a jar of strawberry jam in his refrigerator.

13. *A Case of Spirits*—The only spirits after Holmes's visitor are the ones that he has been drinking. He celebrated the holiday by getting drunk, which affected his perception and made him think that he was seeing a ghost. That "ghost" was only his own reflection in the windows of buildings.

14. *The Case of the Cheap Déjà Vu*—This was not the second time that Professor Flake had visited Holmes, but actually the *third time*! His déjà vu experiences in the story and at other times are a product of his almost—but not completely—forgotten memories. His "déjà vu" experience in Holmes's office is "cheap" because he does not want to remember more than one visit and thus the need to pay for more than one.

15. *The Case of Life or Death*—The solution to this case is open to discussion. Since the Oge Retla are very much like Earth people ("Oge Retla" and "Htrae" are "alter ego" and "Earth" spelled backwards), perhaps Holmes XIII and the students need to consider what they would do if they were in the same position as the Oge Retla—cause the other people to die or make it possible for them to live?

16. *The Case of Life or LIFE*—This is an extension of the preceding case, and it is open to a similar discussion. Mixed feelings are expressed in the taped message, but six of the ten sections (3, 4, 5, 6, 9, and 10) suggest that the speaker wants the Earth people to live. The last two positive expressions are particularly significant because they come at the end and because they suggest that the speaker wants the Earth people to live better, to truly LIVE, by not opening any vault. He suggests that the vault containing nuclear fuel leads ultimately to death.